Ge

NEW INTERNATIONAL VERSION

Introduction and notes by
DAVID PRIOR

Hodder & Stoughton
LONDON SYDNEY AUCKLAND

First published 1995

You will be pleased to know that a portion of the purchase price of your new NIV Gospel has been allocated to the International Bible Society to help spread the Gospel of Jesus Christ around the world.

ISBN 0 340 65172 5

British Library Cataloguing in Publication Data
A record of this book is available in the British Library

Designed and typeset by Kenneth Burnley at Irby, Wirral, Cheshire.
Printed in Great Britain for
Hodder & Stoughton, 338 Euston Road, London NW1 3BH,
by Cox & Wyman Ltd, Reading, Berks

Introduction

As he makes plain at the outset, Luke wants to write an orderly, reliable account of the life, death and resurrection of Jesus Christ. Luke was a master of the Greek language and the original text of his gospel is clearly the work of a well-educated, articulate man. He is writing for an otherwise unknown person called Theophilus and this gospel is Part 1 of a two-volume set about what Jesus came to do and to teach. The second volume is the Acts of the Apostles.

The theme of the gospel is salvation, summed up in the words of Jesus about himself in chapter 19, verse 10: 'The Son of Man came to seek and to save what was lost.' The gospel begins with two chapters which describe the remarkable events surrounding the birth of Jesus to Mary. The emphasis is on the intervention of the Holy Spirit in the lives of ordinary people – a theme which remains uppermost in the next two chapters, in which the beginning of Jesus' public ministry is described.

After Jesus has made his own mission statement in his local synagogue at Nazareth (4:16–21), Luke records incident after incident in which Jesus brings 'good news to the poor' – those who are sick or rejected, those who are in despair or facing death, those who have fallen foul of people in authority – particularly the religious authorities. Luke shows a particular interest in the place of women in the life and ministry of Jesus. He also stresses the priority of prayer.

One of the favourite titles Jesus uses for himself is 'the Son of Man', which is possibly taken from Old Testament descriptions of a future victorious leader who will usher in the kingdom of God. Luke records many of the parables of Jesus – stories which Jesus told to illustrate his teaching about God's kingdom.

The public ministry of Jesus lasted only three years and Luke highlights the growing conflict with the scribes and Pharisees – religious leaders who increasingly saw in Jesus a threat to their influence over ordinary people. There is a key occasion (recorded in chapter 9) after which Jesus begins to spell out to his disciples that his mission will end in his death. From that point he repeatedly tries to get them ready for this violent conclusion to his life.

Luke devotes considerable time to the events leading up to the betrayal, arrest, trial and crucifixion of Jesus. The gospel moves to a powerful climax, as the resurrection of Jesus is described. It ends with a firm note of expectation, as Jesus promises his disciples that they will soon receive the gift of the Holy Spirit, so that they will then be able to take the good news of salvation far and wide throughout the whole world – a reality which Luke goes on to describe in the Acts of the Apostles.

David Prior

Luke's *Gospel*

Luke

Introduction

1 Many have undertaken to draw up an account
of the things that have been fulfilled among
us, 2just as they were handed down to us by those
who from the first were eye-witnesses and ser-
vants of the word. 3Therefore, since I myself
have carefully investigated everything from the
beginning, it seemed good also to me to write an
orderly account for you, most excellent
Theophilus, 4so that you may know the certainty
of the things you have been taught.

Luke explains the background and the purpose of his gospel.

The Birth of John the Baptist Foretold

5In the time of Herod king of Judea there was a
priest named Zechariah, who belonged to the
priestly division of Abijah; his wife Elizabeth
was also a descendant of Aaron. 6Both of them
were upright in the sight of God, observing all
the Lord's commandments and regulations
blamelessly. 7But they had no children, because
Elizabeth was barren; and they were both well
on in years.

8Once when Zechariah's division was on duty
and he was serving as priest before God, 9he was
chosen by lot, according to the custom of the
priesthood, to go into the temple of the Lord
and burn incense. 10And when the time for the
burning of incense came, all the assembled wor-
shippers were praying outside.

11Then an angel of the Lord appeared to him,
standing at the right side of the altar of incense.

Zechariah, a priest on duty in the temple at Jerusalem, sees the angel Gabriel standing by the altar of incense. Gabriel explains to the startled priest that he and his wife, Elizabeth, will have a son in their old age – in spite of years of barrenness. This son (to be called John) is destined to have a powerful ministry as a prophet to the people 'in the spirit and power of Elijah'.

12When Zechariah saw him, he was startled and was gripped with fear. 13But the angel said to him: "Do not be afraid, Zechariah; your prayer has been heard. Your wife Elizabeth will bear you a son, and you are to give him the name John. 14He will be a joy and delight to you, and many will rejoice because of his birth, 15for he will be great in the sight of the Lord. He is never to take wine or other fermented drink, and he will be filled with the Holy Spirit even from birth. 16Many of the people of Israel will he bring back to the Lord their God. 17And he will go on before the Lord, in the spirit and power of Elijah, to turn the hearts of the fathers to their children and the disobedient to the wisdom of the righteous—to make ready a people prepared for the Lord."

18Zechariah asked the angel, "How can I be sure of this? I am an old man and my wife is well on in years."

Zechariah cannot believe it and is told that he will be unable to speak until the child's birth.

19The angel answered, "I am Gabriel. I stand in the presence of God, and I have been sent to speak to you and to tell you this good news. 20And now you will be silent and not able to speak until the day this happens, because you did not believe my words, which will come true at their proper time."

21Meanwhile, the people were waiting for Zechariah and wondering why he stayed so long in the temple. 22When he came out, he could not speak to them. They realised he had seen a vision in the temple, for he kept making signs to them but remained unable to speak.

23When his time of service was completed, he returned home. 24After this his wife Elizabeth became pregnant and for five months remained in seclusion. 25"The Lord has done this for me,"

she said. "In these days he has shown his favour
and taken away my disgrace among the people."

The Birth of Jesus Foretold

[26]In the sixth month, God sent the angel
Gabriel to Nazareth, a town in Galilee, [27]to a
virgin pledged to be married to a man named
Joseph, a descendant of David. The virgin's
name was Mary. [28]The angel went to her and
said, "Greetings, you who are highly favoured!
The Lord is with you."

[29]Mary was greatly troubled at his words and
wondered what kind of greeting this might be.
[30]But the angel said to her, "Do not be afraid,
Mary, you have found favour with God. [31]You
will be with child and give birth to a son, and you
are to give him the name Jesus. [32]He will be
great and will be called the Son of the Most
High. The Lord God will give him the throne of
his father David, [33]and he will reign over the
house of Jacob for ever; his kingdom will never
end."

[34]"How will this be," Mary asked the angel,
"since I am a virgin?"

[35]The angel answered, "The Holy Spirit will
come upon you, and the power of the Most High
will overshadow you. So the holy one to be born
will be called the Son of God. [36]Even Elizabeth
your relative is going to have a child in her old
age, and she who was said to be barren is in her
sixth month. [37]For nothing is impossible with
God."

[38]"I am the Lord's servant," Mary answered.
"May it be to me as you have said." Then the
angel left her.

The angel Gabriel appears to a virgin, called Mary and related to Elizabeth, and tells her that she will bear a son (to be called Jesus), not through normal human conception, but by the power of the Holy Spirit. Her son is destined to fulfil all God's promises to David and to the people of Israel. Unlike Zechariah, Mary accepts this astonishing promise.

Mary Visits Elizabeth

The Holy Spirit inspires Elizabeth to speak with prophetic insight about the child in Mary's womb.

39 At that time Mary got ready and hurried to a
town in the hill country of Judea, 40 where she
entered Zechariah's home and greeted Eliza-
beth. 41 When Elizabeth heard Mary's greeting,
the baby leaped in her womb, and Elizabeth was
filled with the Holy Spirit. 42 In a loud voice she
exclaimed: "Blessed are you among women, and
blessed is the child you will bear! 43 But why am I
so favoured, that the mother of my Lord should
come to me? 44 As soon as the sound of your
greeting reached my ears, the baby in my womb
leaped for joy. 45 Blessed is she who has believed
that what the Lord has said to her will be accom-
plished!"

Mary's Song

46 And Mary said:

Mary expresses her joy and wonder at the astonishing events which are beginning to take place.

"My soul glorifies the Lord
47 and my spirit rejoices in God my Saviour,
48 for he has been mindful
of the humble state of his servant.
From now on all generations will call me
blessed,
49 for the Mighty One has done great things for
me—
holy is his name.
50 His mercy extends to those who fear him,
from generation to generation.
51 He has performed mighty deeds with his arm;
he has scattered those who are proud in
their inmost thoughts.
52 He has brought down rulers from their
thrones
but has lifted up the humble.

53He has filled the hungry with good things
but has sent the rich away empty.
54He has helped his servant Israel,
remembering to be merciful
55to Abraham and his descendants for ever,
even as he said to our fathers."

56Mary stayed with Elizabeth for about three
months and then returned home.

The Birth of John the Baptist

57When it was time for Elizabeth to have her
baby, she gave birth to a son. 58Her neighbours
and relatives heard that the Lord had shown her
great mercy, and they shared her joy.
59On the eighth day they came to circumcise
the child, and they were going to name him after
his father Zechariah, 60but his mother spoke up
and said, "No! He is to be called John."
61They said to her, "There is no-one among
your relatives who has that name."
62Then they made signs to his father, to find
out what he would like to name the child. 63He
asked for a writing tablet, and to everyone's
astonishment he wrote, "His name is John."
64Immediately his mouth was opened and his
tongue was loosed, and he began to speak, praising God. 65The neighbours were all filled with
awe, and throughout the hill country of Judea
people were talking about all these things.
66Everyone who heard this wondered about it,
asking, "What then is this child going to be?"
For the Lord's hand was with him.

When Elizabeth produces a son, Zechariah confirms in writing that his name is to be John and immediately he is able to speak again. His first words are full of praise to God.

Zechariah's Song

The Holy Spirit inspires Zechariah to foretell a dramatic ministry for his son – as a prophet preparing the way for the Lord to visit his people.

67His father Zechariah was filled with the Holy Spirit and prophesied:

68"Praise be to the Lord, the God of Israel,
because he has come and has redeemed his people.
69He has raised up a horn of salvation for us
in the house of his servant David
70(as he said through his holy prophets of long ago),
71salvation from our enemies
and from the hand of all who hate us—
72to show mercy to our fathers
and to remember his holy covenant,
73 the oath he swore to our father Abraham:
74to rescue us from the hand of our enemies,
and to enable us to serve him without fear
75 in holiness and righteousness before him all our days.

76And you, my child, will be called a prophet of the Most High;
for you will go on before the Lord to prepare the way for him,
77to give his people the knowledge of salvation
through the forgiveness of their sins,
78because of the tender mercy of our God,
by which the rising sun will come to us from heaven
79to shine on those living in darkness
and in the shadow of death,
to guide our feet into the path of peace."

80And the child grew and became strong in spirit; and he lived in the desert until he appeared publicly to Israel.

The Birth of Jesus

2 In those days Caesar Augustus issued a
decree that a census should be taken of the
entire Roman world. (2This was the first census
that took place while Quirinius was governor of
Syria.) 3And everyone went to his own town to
register.

4So Joseph also went up from the town of
Nazareth in Galilee to Judea, to Bethlehem the
town of David, because he belonged to the
house and line of David. 5He went there to
register with Mary, who was pledged to be mar-
ried to him and was expecting a child. 6While
they were there, the time came for the baby to be
born, 7and she gave birth to her firstborn, a son.
She wrapped him in cloths and placed him in a
manger, because there was no room for them in
the inn.

Mary gives birth to her son in a manger at Bethlehem.

The Shepherds and the Angels

8And there were shepherds living out in the
fields near by, keeping watch over their flocks at
night. 9An angel of the Lord appeared to them,
and the glory of the Lord shone around them,
and they were terrified. 10But the angel said to
them, "Do not be afraid. I bring you good news
of great joy that will be for all the people.
11Today in the town of David a Saviour has been
born to you; he is Christ the Lord. 12This will be
a sign to you: You will find a baby wrapped in
cloths and lying in a manger."

13Suddenly a great company of the heavenly
host appeared with the angel, praising God and
saying,

That same night an angel appears to shepherds in the fields and tells them about the birth of a Saviour in nearby Bethlehem. Good news which is then expressed in glorious praise by a great company of angelic beings.

14“Glory to God in the highest,
and on earth peace to men on whom his
favour rests.”

The shepherds hurry to Bethlehem to find the baby.

15When the angels had left them and gone into
heaven, the shepherds said to one another,
“Let's go to Bethlehem and see this thing that
has happened, which the Lord has told us
about.”
16So they hurried off and found Mary and
Joseph, and the baby, who was lying in the
manger. 17When they had seen him, they spread
the word concerning what had been told them
about this child, 18and all who heard it were
amazed at what the shepherds said to them.
19But Mary treasured up all these things and
pondered them in her heart. 20The shepherds
returned, glorifying and praising God for all the
things they had heard and seen, which were just
as they had been told.

Jesus Presented in the Temple

Mary and Joseph take Jesus to the temple of Jerusalem, where the Holy Spirit enables a devout old man, Simeon, to see the true identity of the baby.

21On the eighth day, when it was time to cir-
cumcise him, he was named Jesus, the name the
angel had given him before he had been con-
ceived.
22When the time of their purification accord-
ing to the Law of Moses had been completed,
Joseph and Mary took him to Jerusalem to
present him to the Lord 23(as it is written in the
Law of the Lord, “Every firstborn male is to be
consecrated to the Lord”), 24and to offer a sacri-
fice in keeping with what is said in the Law of the
Lord: “a pair of doves or two young pigeons”.
25Now there was a man in Jerusalem called
Simeon, who was righteous and devout. He was
waiting for the consolation of Israel, and the

Holy Spirit was upon him. [26]It had been
revealed to him by the Holy Spirit that he would
not die before he had seen the Lord's Christ.
[27]Moved by the Spirit, he went into the temple
courts. When the parents brought in the child
Jesus to do for him what the custom of the Law
required, [28]Simeon took him in his arms and
praised God, saying:

[29]"Sovereign Lord, as you have promised,
you now dismiss your servant in peace.
[30]For my eyes have seen your salvation,
[31] which you have prepared in the sight of
all people,
[32]a light for revelation to the Gentiles
and for glory to your people Israel."

[33]The child's father and mother marvelled at
what was said about him. [34]Then Simeon
blessed them and said to Mary, his mother:
"This child is destined to cause the falling and
rising of many in Israel, and to be a sign that will
be spoken against, [35]so that the thoughts of
many hearts will be revealed. And a sword will
pierce your own soul too."

Mary and Joseph, already taken aback by what Simeon says about the child, now hear more about what lies ahead for him and for them.

[36]There was also a prophetess, Anna, the
daughter of Phanuel, of the tribe of Asher. She
was very old; she had lived with her husband
seven years after her marriage, [37]and then was a
widow until she was eighty-four. She never left
the temple but worshipped night and day, fast-
ing and praying. [38]Coming up to them at that
very moment, she gave thanks to God and spoke
about the child to all who were looking forward
to the redemption of Jerusalem.

[39]When Joseph and Mary had done every-
thing required by the Law of the Lord, they

returned to Galilee to their own town of
Nazareth. 40And the child grew and became
strong; he was filled with wisdom, and the grace
of God was upon him.

The Boy Jesus at the Temple

Jesus, now twelve years old, astonishes the religious teachers of the temple with his understanding. Returning home to Nazareth, he grows in wisdom and reputation.

41Every year his parents went to Jerusalem for
the Feast of the Passover. 42When he was twelve
years old, they went up to the Feast, according
to the custom. 43After the Feast was over, while
his parents were returning home, the boy Jesus
stayed behind in Jerusalem, but they were
unaware of it. 44Thinking he was in their com-
pany, they travelled on for a day. Then they
began looking for him among their relatives and
friends. 45When they did not find him, they
went back to Jerusalem to look for him. 46After
three days they found him in the temple courts,
sitting among the teachers, listening to them
and asking them questions. 47Everyone who
heard him was amazed at his understanding and
his answers. 48When his parents saw him, they
were astonished. His mother said to him, "Son,
why have you treated us like this? Your father
and I have been anxiously searching for you."

49"Why were you searching for me?" he asked.
"Didn't you know I had to be in my Father's
house?" 50But they did not understand what he
was saying to them.

51Then he went down to Nazareth with them
and was obedient to them. But his mother treas-
ured all these things in her heart. 52And Jesus
grew in wisdom and stature, and in favour with
God and men.

John the Baptist Prepares the Way

3 In the fifteenth year of the reign of Tiberius
Caesar—when Pontius Pilate was governor
of Judea, Herod tetrarch of Galilee, his brother
Philip tetrarch of Iturea and Traconitis, and
Lysanias tetrarch of Abilene—2during the high
priesthood of Annas and Caiaphas, the word of
God came to John son of Zechariah in the
desert. 3He went into all the country around the
Jordan, preaching a baptism of repentance for
the forgiveness of sins. 4As is written in the book
of the words of Isaiah the prophet:

Luke moves on a further fifteen years or so and describes the dramatic impact of John the Baptist as he calls on people to repent. He is now preparing the way for the Lord's arrival, by baptising them in the River Jordan.

"A voice of one calling in the desert,
'Prepare the way for the Lord,
make straight paths for him.
5Every valley shall be filled in,
every mountain and hill made low.
The crooked roads shall become straight,
the rough ways smooth.
6And all mankind will see God's salvation.'"

7John said to the crowds coming out to be
baptised by him, "You brood of vipers! Who
warned you to flee from the coming wrath?
8Produce fruit in keeping with repentance. And
do not begin to say to yourselves, 'We have
Abraham as our father.' For I tell you that out of
these stones God can raise up children for Abra-
ham. 9The axe is already at the root of the trees,
and every tree that does not produce good fruit
will be cut down and thrown into the fire."

10"What should we do then?" the crowd
asked.

11John answered, "The man with two tunics
should share with him who has none, and the
one who has food should do the same."

12 Tax collectors also came to be baptised. "Teacher," they asked, "what should we do?"

13 "Don't collect any more than you are required to," he told them.

14 Then some soldiers asked him, "And what should we do?"

He replied, "Don't extort money and don't accuse people falsely—be content with your pay."

When the people start wondering whether John might be the long-awaited Messiah, John swiftly points away from himself to someone more powerful, who will baptise people with the fire of the Holy Spirit.

15 The people were waiting expectantly and were all wondering in their hearts if John might possibly be the Christ. 16 John answered them all, "I baptise you with water. But one more powerful than I will come, the thongs of whose sandals I am not worthy to untie. He will baptise you with the Holy Spirit and with fire. 17 His winnowing fork is in his hand to clear his threshing-floor and to gather the wheat into his barn, but he will burn up the chaff with unquenchable fire." 18 And with many other words John exhorted the people and preached the good news to them.

19 But when John rebuked Herod the tetrarch because of Herodias, his brother's wife, and all the other evil things he had done, 20 Herod added this to them all: He locked John up in prison.

The Baptism and Genealogy of Jesus

The Holy Spirit visibly descends on Jesus, as he is baptised in the Jordan by John, and a voice from heaven identifies Jesus as God's Son.

21 When all the people were being baptised, Jesus was baptised too. And as he was praying, heaven was opened 22 and the Holy Spirit descended on him in bodily form like a dove. And a voice came from heaven: "You are my Son, whom I love; with you I am well pleased."

23 Now Jesus himself was about thirty years old when he began his ministry. He was the son, so it was thought, of Joseph,

the son of Heli, 24 the son of Matthat,
the son of Levi, the son of Melki,
the son of Jannai, the son of Joseph,
25 the son of Mattathias, the son of Amos,
the son of Nahum, the son of Esli,
the son of Naggai, 26 the son of Maath,
the son of Mattathias, the son of Semein,
the son of Josech, the son of Joda,
27 the son of Joanan, the son of Rhesa,
the son of Zerubbabel, the son of Shealtiel,
the son of Neri, 28 the son of Melki,
the son of Addi, the son of Cosam,
the son of Elmadam, the son of Er,
29 the son of Joshua, the son of Eliezer,
the son of Jorim, the son of Matthat,
the son of Levi, 30 the son of Simeon,
the son of Judah, the son of Joseph,
the son of Jonam, the son of Eliakim,
31 the son of Melea, the son of Menna,
the son of Mattatha, the son of Nathan,
the son of David, 32 the son of Jesse,
the son of Obed, the son of Boaz,
the son of Salmon, the son of Nahshon,
33 the son of Amminadab, the son of Ram,
the son of Hezron, the son of Perez,
the son of Judah, 34 the son of Jacob,
the son of Isaac, the son of Abraham,
the son of Terah, the son of Nahor,
35 the son of Serug, the son of Reu,
the son of Peleg, the son of Eber,
the son of Shelah, 36 the son of Cainan,
the son of Arphaxad, the son of Shem,
the son of Noah, the son of Lamech,
37 the son of Methuselah, the son of Enoch,
the son of Jared, the son of Mahalalel,
the son of Kenan, 38 the son of Enosh,
the son of Seth, the son of Adam,
the son of God.

Jesus' family tree, on Joseph's side, is traced back through the generations to David, Jacob, Abraham and Adam. Here Luke seems to be emphasising the humanness of Jesus.

The Temptation of Jesus

The Holy Spirit leads Jesus out into the wilderness, where after forty days and nights without any food, he is fiercely tempted by the devil. Jesus emerges triumphant by looking to God and trusting in God's Word.

4 Jesus, full of the Holy Spirit, returned from
the Jordan and was led by the Spirit in the
desert, [2]where for forty days he was tempted by
the devil. He ate nothing during those days, and
at the end of them he was hungry.

[3]The devil said to him, "If you are the Son of
God, tell this stone to become bread."

[4]Jesus answered, "It is written: 'Man does not
live on bread alone.'"

[5]The devil led him up to a high place and
showed him in an instant all the kingdoms of the
world. [6]And he said to him, "I will give you all
their authority and splendour, for it has been
given to me, and I can give it to anyone I want to.
[7]So if you worship me, it will all be yours."

[8]Jesus answered, "It is written: 'Worship the
Lord your God and serve him only.'"

[9]The devil led him to Jerusalem and had him
stand on the highest point of the temple. "If you
are the Son of God," he said, "throw yourself
down from here. [10]For it is written:

"'He will command his angels concerning you
to guard you carefully;
[11]they will lift you up in their hands,
so that you will not strike your foot
against a stone.'"

[12]Jesus answered, "It says: 'Do not put the
Lord your God to the test.'"[13]When the devil
had finished all this tempting, he left him until
an opportune time.

Jesus Rejected at Nazareth

[14]Jesus returned to Galilee in the power of the
Spirit, and news about him spread through the

whole countryside. [15]He taught in their syna-
gogues, and everyone praised him.

[16]He went to Nazareth, where he had been
brought up, and on the Sabbath day he went
into the synagogue, as was his custom. And he
stood up to read. [17]The scroll of the prophet
Isaiah was handed to him. Unrolling it, he found
the place where it is written:

In his home town Jesus spells out his mission – to preach good news to the poor in the power of the Holy Spirit. His own people turn against him and almost murder him.

[18]"The Spirit of the Lord is on me,
because he has anointed me
to preach good news to the poor.
He has sent me to proclaim freedom for the
prisoners
and recovery of sight for the blind,
to release the oppressed,
19 to proclaim the year of the Lord's favour."

[20]Then he rolled up the scroll, gave it back to
the attendant and sat down. The eyes of every-
one in the synagogue were fastened on him,
[21]and he began by saying to them, "Today this
scripture is fulfilled in your hearing."

[22]All spoke well of him and were amazed at the
gracious words that came from his lips. "Isn't
this Joseph's son?" they asked.

[23]Jesus said to them, "Surely you will quote
this proverb to me: 'Physician, heal yourself! Do
here in your home town what we have heard
that you did in Capernaum.'"

[24]"I tell you the truth," he continued, "no
prophet is accepted in his home town. [25]I assure
you that there were many widows in Israel in
Elijah's time, when the sky was shut for three
and a half years and there was a severe famine
throughout the land. [26]Yet Elijah was not sent to
any of them, but to a widow in Zarephath in the

region of Sidon. 27And there were many in Israel
with leprosy in the time of Elisha the prophet,
yet not one of them was cleansed—only
Naaman the Syrian."

28All the people in the synagogue were furious
when they heard this. 29They got up, drove him
out of the town, and took him to the brow of the
hill on which the town was built, in order to
throw him down the cliff. 30But he walked right
through the crowd and went on his way.

Jesus Drives Out an Evil Spirit

Moving on to Capernaum, Jesus reveals his authority over evil forces controlling the life of a worshipper in the local synagogue.

31Then he went down to Capernaum, a town
in Galilee, and on the Sabbath began to teach
the people. 32They were amazed at his teaching,
because his message had authority.

33In the synagogue there was a man possessed
by a demon, an evil spirit. He cried out at the top
of his voice, 34"Ha! What do you want with us,
Jesus of Nazareth? Have you come to destroy
us? I know who you are—the Holy One of
God!"

35"Be quiet!" Jesus said sternly. "Come out of
him!" Then the demon threw the man down
before them all and came out without injuring
him.

36All the people were amazed and said to each
other, "What is this teaching? With authority
and power he gives orders to evil spirits and they
come out!" 37And the news about him spread
throughout the surrounding area.

Jesus Heals Many

38Jesus left the synagogue and went to the
home of Simon. Now Simon's mother-in-law
was suffering from a high fever, and they asked

Jesus to help her. 39So he bent over her and rebuked the fever, and it left her. She got up at once and began to wait on them.

40When the sun was setting, the people brought to Jesus all who had various kinds of sickness, and laying his hands on each one, he healed them. 41Moreover, demons came out of many people, shouting, "You are the Son of God!" But he rebuked them and would not allow them to speak, because they knew he was the Christ.

42At daybreak Jesus went out to a solitary place. The people were looking for him and when they came to where he was, they tried to keep him from leaving them. 43But he said, "I must preach the good news of the kingdom of God to the other towns also, because that is why I was sent." 44And he kept on preaching in the synagogues of Judea.

His healing powers begin to cause quite a stir. Many people are healed, but Jesus insists on moving on to other towns, teaching and preaching.

The Calling of the First Disciples

5 One day as Jesus was standing by the Lake of Gennesaret, with the people crowding round him and listening to the word of God, 2he saw at the water's edge two boats, left there by the fishermen, who were washing their nets. 3He got into one of the boats, the one belonging to Simon, and asked him to put out a little from shore. Then he sat down and taught the people from the boat.

4When he had finished speaking, he said to Simon, "Put out into deep water, and let down the nets for a catch."

5Simon answered, "Master, we've worked hard all night and haven't caught anything. But because you say so, I will let down the nets."

Jesus begins to select particular individuals to be his disciples, beginning with Simon Peter, James and John – all fishermen.

6When they had done so, they caught such a
large number of fish that their nets began to
break. 7So they signalled to their partners in the
other boat to come and help them, and they
came and filled both boats so full that they began
to sink.

8When Simon Peter saw this, he fell at Jesus'
knees and said, "Go away from me, Lord; I am a
sinful man!" 9For he and all his companions
were astonished at the catch of fish they had
taken, 10and so were James and John, the sons of
Zebedee, Simon's partners.

Then Jesus said to Simon, "Don't be afraid;
from now on you will catch men." 11So they
pulled their boats up on shore, left everything
and followed him.

The Man With Leprosy

In his mission to the poor, Jesus shows special concern for a leper – one of the rejects of his society.

12While Jesus was in one of the towns, a man
came along who was covered with leprosy.
When he saw Jesus, he fell with his face to the
ground and begged him, "Lord, if you are will-
ing, you can make me clean."

13Jesus reached out his hand and touched the
man. "I am willing," he said. "Be clean!" And
immediately the leprosy left him.

14Then Jesus ordered him, "Don't tell anyone,
but go, show yourself to the priest and offer the
sacrifices that Moses commanded for your
cleansing, as a testimony to them."

15Yet the news about him spread all the more,
so that crowds of people came to hear him and to
be healed of their sicknesses. 16But Jesus often
withdrew to lonely places and prayed.

Jesus Heals a Paralytic

17One day as he was teaching, Pharisees and
teachers of the law, who had come from every
village of Galilee and from Judea and Jerusalem,
were sitting there. And the power of the Lord
was present for him to heal the sick. 18Some men
came carrying a paralytic on a mat and tried to
take him into the house to lay him before Jesus.
19When they could not find a way to do this
because of the crowd, they went up on the roof
and lowered him on his mat through the tiles
into the middle of the crowd, right in front of
Jesus.

20When Jesus saw their faith, he said, "Friend,
your sins are forgiven."

21The Pharisees and the teachers of the law
began thinking to themselves, "Who is this fellow who speaks blasphemy? Who can forgive
sins but God alone?"

22Jesus knew what they were thinking and
asked, "Why are you thinking these things in
your hearts? 23Which is easier: to say, 'Your sins
are forgiven,' or to say, 'Get up and walk'? 24But
that you may know that the Son of Man has
authority on earth to forgive sins. . . ." He said to
the paralysed man, "I tell you, get up, take your
mat and go home." 25Immediately he stood up
in front of them, took what he had been lying on
and went home praising God. 26Everyone was
amazed and gave praise to God. They were
filled with awe and said, "We have seen remarkable things today."

Controversy begins to emerge, as Jesus links his power to heal with the authority to forgive sins. The Pharisees, an influential religious group, start to watch Jesus closely.

The Calling of Levi

Jesus chooses another disciple, Levi (or Matthew) from one of the most hated sections of Jewish society: the tax collectors, who made a lot of money by working for the detested Roman occupying forces.

27After this, Jesus went out and saw a tax collector by the name of Levi sitting at his tax booth. "Follow me," Jesus said to him, 28and Levi got up, left everything and followed him.

29Then Levi held a great banquet for Jesus at his house, and a large crowd of tax collectors and others were eating with them. 30But the Pharisees and the teachers of the law who belonged to their sect complained to his disciples, "Why do you eat and drink with tax collectors and 'sinners'?"

31Jesus answered them, "It is not the healthy who need a doctor, but the sick. 32I have not come to call the righteous, but sinners to repentance."

Jesus Questioned About Fasting

Because Jesus is not following all the negative dos and don'ts of the Pharisees, he has to explain that he has come to provide 'new wine'. This means celebration, not long faces.

33They said to him, "John's disciples often fast and pray, and so do the disciples of the Pharisees, but yours go on eating and drinking."

34Jesus answered, "Can you make the guests of the bridegroom fast while he is with them? 35But the time will come when the bridegroom will be taken from them; in those days they will fast."

36He told them this parable: "No-one tears a patch from a new garment and sews it on an old one. If he does, he will have torn the new garment, and the patch from the new will not match the old. 37And no-one pours new wine into old wineskins. If he does, the new wine will burst the skins, the wine will run out and the wineskins will be ruined. 38No, new wine must be poured into new wineskins. 39And no-one after drinking old wine wants the new, for he says, 'The old is better.'"

Lord of the Sabbath

6 One Sabbath Jesus was going through the
cornfields, and his disciples began to pick
some ears of corn, rub them in their hands and
eat the grain. 2Some of the Pharisees asked,
"Why are you doing what is unlawful on the
Sabbath?"
3Jesus answered them, "Have you never read
what David did when he and his companions
were hungry? 4He entered the house of God,
and taking the consecrated bread, he ate what is
lawful only for priests to eat. And he also gave
some to his companions." 5Then Jesus said to
them, "The Son of Man is Lord of the Sabbath."
6On another Sabbath he went into the syna-
gogue and was teaching, and a man was there
whose right hand was shrivelled. 7The Pharisees
and the teachers of the law were looking for a
reason to accuse Jesus, so they watched him
closely to see if he would heal on the Sabbath.
8But Jesus knew what they were thinking and
said to the man with the shrivelled hand, "Get
up and stand in front of everyone." So he got up
and stood there.
9Then Jesus said to them, "I ask you, which is
lawful on the Sabbath: to do good or to do evil,
to save life or to destroy it?"
10He looked round at them all, and then said to
the man, "Stretch out your hand." He did so,
and his hand was completely restored. 11But
they were furious and began to discuss with one
another what they might do to Jesus.

The Pharisees again criticise Jesus for not abiding by their rules and regulations, this time about the Sabbath. Jesus stresses the spirit of such laws, not the letter, by healing the withered hand of a man in the synagogue.

The Twelve Apostles

12One of those days Jesus went out to a moun-
tainside to pray, and spent the night praying to

After a night of prayer, Jesus chooses his team of twelve disciples to share in his mission.

God. 13 When morning came, he called his dis-
ciples to him and chose twelve of them, whom
he also designated apostles: 14 Simon (whom he
named Peter), his brother Andrew, James, John,
Philip, Bartholomew 15 Matthew, Thomas,
James son of Alphaeus, Simon who was called
the Zealot, 16 Judas son of James, and Judas Iscar-
iot, who became a traitor.

Jesus continues to teach, preach, heal the sick and set people free from evil forces.

17 He went down with them and stood on a
level place. A large crowd of his disciples was
there and a great number of people from all over
Judea, from Jerusalem, and from the coast of
Tyre and Sidon, 18 who had come to hear him
and to be healed of their diseases. Those trou-
bled by evil spirits were cured 19 and the people
all tried to touch him, because power was com-
ing from him and healing them all.

20 Looking at his disciples, he said:

Jesus lays down basic principles and guidelines for his disciples in their daily lives.

"Blessed are you who are poor,
  for yours is the kingdom of God.
21 Blessed are you who hunger now,
  for you will be satisfied.
Blessed are you who weep now,
  for you will laugh.
22 Blessed are you when men hate you,
  when they exclude you and insult you
  and reject your name as evil,
  because of the Son of Man.

23 "Rejoice in that day and leap for joy, because
great is your reward in heaven. For that is how
their fathers treated the prophets.

24 "But woe to you who are rich,
  for you have already received your comfort.
25 Woe to you who are well fed now,

for you will go hungry.
Woe to you who laugh now,
for you will mourn and weep.
26Woe to you when all men speak well of you,
for that is how their fathers treated the
false prophets.

Love for Enemies

27"But I tell you who hear me: Love your enemies, do good to those who hate you, 28bless those who curse you, pray for those who ill-treat you. 29If someone strikes you on one cheek, turn to him the other also. If someone takes your cloak, do not stop him from taking your tunic. 30Give to everyone who asks you, and if anyone takes what belongs to you, do not demand it back. 31Do to others as you would have them do to you.

Jesus emphasises his call to his followers to be different.

32"If you love those who love you, what credit is that to you? Even 'sinners' love those who love them. 33And if you do good to those who are good to you, what credit is that to you? Even 'sinners' do that. 34And if you lend to those from whom you expect repayment, what credit is that to you? Even 'sinners' lend to 'sinners', expecting to be repaid in full. 35But love your enemies, do good to them, and lend to them without expecting to get anything back. Then your reward will be great, and you will be sons of the Most High, because he is kind to the ungrateful and wicked. 36Be merciful, just as your Father is merciful.

Judging Others

37"Do not judge, and you will not be judged. Do not condemn, and you will not be con-

He underlines the importance of humility and generosity.

demned. Forgive, and you will be forgiven.
38Give, and it will be given to you. A good meas-
ure, pressed down, shaken together and running
over, will be poured into your lap. For with the
measure you use, it will be measured to you."
39He also told them this parable: "Can a blind
man lead a blind man? Will they not both fall
into a pit? 40A student is not above his teacher,
but everyone who is fully trained will be like his
teacher.
41"Why do you look at the speck of sawdust in
your brother's eye and pay no attention to the
plank in your own eye? 42How can you say to
your brother, 'Brother, let me take the speck out
of your eye,' when you yourself fail to see the
plank in your own eye? You hypocrite, first take
the plank out of your eye, and then you will see
clearly to remove the speck from your brother's
eye.

A Tree and Its Fruit

He focuses on the state of our hearts, because everything else springs from there.

43"No good tree bears bad fruit, nor does a bad
tree bear good fruit. 44Each tree is recognised by
its own fruit. People do not pick figs from thorn-
bushes, or grapes from briers. 45The good man
brings good things out of the good stored up in
his heart, and the evil man brings evil things out
of the evil stored up in his heart. For out of the
overflow of his heart his mouth speaks.

The Wise and Foolish Builders

He makes us examine the true foundation of our lives.

46"Why do you call me, 'Lord, Lord,' and do
not do what I say? 47I will show you what he is
like who comes to me and hears my words and
puts them into practice. 48He is like a man build-
ing a house, who dug down deep and laid the

foundation on rock. When the flood came, the torrent struck that house but could not shake it, because it was well built. 49But the one who hears my words and does not put them into practice is like a man who built a house on the ground without a foundation. The moment the torrent struck that house, it collapsed and its destruction was complete."

The Faith of the Centurion

7 When Jesus had finished saying all this in the hearing of the people, he entered Capernaum. 2There a centurion's servant, whom his master valued highly, was sick and about to die. 3The centurion heard of Jesus and sent some elders of the Jews to him, asking him to come and heal his servant. 4When they came to Jesus, they pleaded earnestly with him, "This man deserves to have you do this, 5because he loves our nation and has built our synagogue." 6So Jesus went with them.

A Roman centurion provides a striking example of what it means to have faith in Jesus.

He was not far from the house when the centurion sent friends to say to him: "Lord, don't trouble yourself, for I do not deserve to have you come under my roof. 7That is why I did not even consider myself worthy to come to you. But say the word, and my servant will be healed. 8For I myself am a man under authority, with soldiers under me. I tell this one, 'Go', and he goes; and that one, 'Come', and he comes. I say to my servant, 'Do this', and he does it."

9When Jesus heard this, he was amazed at him, and turning to the crowd following him, he said, "I tell you, I have not found such great faith even in Israel." 10Then the men who had been sent returned to the house and found the servant well.

Jesus Raises a Widow's Son

A young man is raised from the dead.

11 Soon afterwards, Jesus went to a town called Nain, and his disciples and a large crowd went along with him. 12 As he approached the town gate, a dead person was being carried out—the only son of his mother, and she was a widow. And a large crowd from the town was with her. 13 When the Lord saw her, his heart went out to her and he said, "Don't cry."

14 Then he went up and touched the coffin, and those carrying it stood still. He said, "Young man, I say to you, get up!" 15 The dead man sat up and began to talk, and Jesus gave him back to his mother.

16 They were all filled with awe and praised God. "A great prophet has appeared among us," they said. "God has come to help his people." 17 This news about Jesus spread throughout Judea and the surrounding country.

Jesus and John the Baptist

In the middle of a very busy period of teaching and healing, Jesus takes time to answer searching questions about himself and his mission. These come from messengers sent to him by John the Baptist, who is now in prison.

18 John's disciples told him about all these things. Calling two of them, 19 he sent them to the Lord to ask, "Are you the one who was to come, or should we expect someone else?"

20 When the men came to Jesus, they said, "John the Baptist sent us to you to ask, 'Are you the one who was to come, or should we expect someone else?'"

21 At that very time Jesus cured many who had diseases, sicknesses and evil spirits, and gave sight to many who were blind. 22 So he replied to the messengers, "Go back and report to John what you have seen and heard: The blind receive sight, the lame walk, those who have leprosy are cured, the deaf hear, the dead are raised, and the

good news is preached to the poor. [23]Blessed is the man who does not fall away on account of me."

[24]After John's messengers left, Jesus began to speak to the crowd about John: "What did you go out into the desert to see? A reed swayed by the wind? [25]If not, what did you go out to see? A man dressed in fine clothes? No, those who wear expensive clothes and indulge in luxury are in palaces. [26]But what did you go out to see? A prophet? Yes, I tell you, and more than a prophet. [27]This is the one about whom it is written:

Jesus explains the importance of John, but goes on to state that John is only a forerunner for his own ministry. The most important thing is to realise that in Jesus himself the kingdom of God has fully arrived.

> "'I will send my messenger ahead of you,
> who will prepare your way before you.'

[28]I tell you, among those born of women there is no-one greater than John; yet the one who is least in the kingdom of God is greater than he."

([29]All the people, even the tax collectors, when they heard Jesus' words, acknowledged that God's way was right, because they had been baptised by John. [30]But the Pharisees and experts in the law rejected God's purpose for themselves, because they had not been baptised by John.)

[31]"To what, then, can I compare the people of this generation? What are they like? [32]They are like children sitting in the market-place and calling out to each other:

> "'We played the flute for you,
> and you did not dance;
> we sang a dirge,
> and you did not cry.'

[33]For John the Baptist came neither eating

bread nor drinking wine, and you say, 'He has a
demon.' 34The Son of Man came eating and
drinking, and you say, 'Here is a glutton and a
drunkard, a friend of tax collectors and "sin-
ners".' 35But wisdom is proved right by all her
children."

Jesus Anointed by a Sinful Woman

A prostitute lavishes loving attention on Jesus, when he is having dinner in the house of Simon the Pharisee. Jesus shows Simon the centrality of his forgiveness and the woman's faith.

36Now one of the Pharisees invited Jesus to
have dinner with him, so he went to the Phar-
isee's house and reclined at the table. 37When a
woman who had lived a sinful life in that town
learned that Jesus was eating at the Pharisee's
house, she brought an alabaster jar of perfume,
38and as she stood behind him at his feet weep-
ing, she began to wet his feet with her tears.
Then she wiped them with her hair, kissed them
and poured perfume on them.

39When the Pharisee who had invited him saw
this, he said to himself, "If this man were a
prophet, he would know who is touching him
and what kind of woman she is—that she is a sin-
ner."

40Jesus answered him, "Simon, I have some-
thing to tell you."

"Tell me, teacher," he said.

41"Two men owed money to a certain money-
lender. One owed him five hundred denarii, and
the other fifty. 42Neither of them had the money
to pay him back, so he cancelled the debts of
both. Now which of them will love him more?"

43Simon replied, "I suppose the one who had
the bigger debt cancelled."

"You have judged correctly," Jesus said.

44Then he turned towards the woman and said
to Simon, "Do you see this woman? I came into

your house. You did not give me any water for my feet, but she wet my feet with her tears and wiped them with her hair. [45]You did not give me a kiss, but this woman, from the time I entered has not stopped kissing my feet. [46]You did not put oil on my head, but she has poured perfume on my feet. [47]Therefore, I tell you, her many sins have been forgiven—for she loved much. But he who has been forgiven little loves little."

[48]Then Jesus said to her, "Your sins are forgiven."

[49]The other guests began to say among themselves, "Who is this who even forgives sins?"

[50]Jesus said to the woman, "Your faith has saved you; go in peace."

The Parable of the Sower

8 After this, Jesus travelled about from one town and village to another, proclaiming the good news of the kingdom of God. The Twelve were with him, [2]and also some women who had been cured of evil spirits and diseases: Mary (called Magdalene) from whom seven demons had come out; [3]Joanna the wife of Chuza, the manager of Herod's household; Susanna; and many others. These women were helping to support them out of their own means.

As Jesus continues his public ministry, Luke describes the valuable support given by several women in his company.

[4]While a large crowd was gathering and people were coming to Jesus from town after town, he told this parable: [5]"A farmer went out to sow his seed. As he was scattering the seed, some fell along the path; it was trampled on, and the birds of the air ate it up. [6]Some fell on rock, and when it came up, the plants withered because they had no moisture. [7]Other seed fell among thorns, which grew up with it and choked the plants.

Jesus often used parables to get across his message. In the parable of the sower, he gives important insights into the different responses people make when they hear the Word of God.

8 Still other seed fell on good soil. It came up and
yielded a crop, a hundred times more than was
sown."
When he said this, he called out, "He who has
ears to hear, let him hear."
9 His disciples asked him what this parable
meant. 10 He said, "The knowledge of the secrets
of the kingdom of God has been given to you,
but to others I speak in parables, so that,

"'though seeing, they may not see;
though hearing, they may not understand.'

11 "This is the meaning of the parable: The
seed is the word of God. 12 Those along the path
are the ones who hear, and then the devil comes
and takes away the word from their hearts, so
that they may not believe and be saved. 13 Those
on the rock are the ones who receive the word
with joy when they hear it, but they have no
root. They believe for a while, but in the time of
testing they fall away. 14 The seed that fell among
thorns stands for those who hear, but as they go
on their way they are choked by life's worries,
riches and pleasures, and they do not mature.
15 But the seed on good soil stands for those with
a noble and good heart, who hear the word,
retain it, and by persevering produce a crop.

A Lamp on a Stand

Jesus again underlines the importance of listening carefully to what he has to say.

16 "No-one lights a lamp and hides it in a jar or
puts it under a bed. Instead, he puts it on a stand,
so that those who come in can see the light.
17 For there is nothing hidden that will not be
disclosed, and nothing concealed that will not be
known or brought out into the open. 18 There-
fore consider carefully how you listen. Whoever

has will be given more; whoever does not have, even what he thinks he has will be taken from him."

Jesus' Mother and Brothers

19Now Jesus' mother and brothers came to see him, but they were not able to get near him because of the crowd. 20Someone told him, "Your mother and brothers are standing outside, wanting to see you."

21He replied, "My mother and brothers are those who hear God's word and put it into practice."

Listening to God's Word and obeying it brings us closer to Jesus than even his own mother and brothers.

Jesus Calms the Storm

22One day Jesus said to his disciples, "Let's go over to the other side of the lake." So they got into a boat and set out. 23As they sailed, he fell asleep. A squall came down on the lake, so that the boat was being swamped, and they were in great danger.

24The disciples went and woke him, saying, "Master, Master, we're going to drown!"

He got up and rebuked the wind and the raging waters; the storm subsided, and all was calm.
25"Where is your faith?" he asked his disciples.

In fear and amazement they asked one another, "Who is this? He commands even the winds and the water, and they obey him."

The disciples are astounded by Jesus' power to calm a storm on the lake.

The Healing of a Demon-possessed Man

26They sailed to the region of the Gerasenes, which is across the lake from Galilee. 27When Jesus stepped ashore, he was met by a demon-possessed man from the town. For a long time this man had not worn clothes or lived in a

Jesus demonstrates his complete authority to calm, free and heal an extremely violent man who has been running wild and untamed for years.

house, but had lived in the tombs. [28]When he
saw Jesus, he cried out and fell at his feet, shout-
ing at the top of his voice, "What do you want
with me, Jesus, Son of the Most High God? I
beg you, don't torture me!" [29]For Jesus had com-
manded the evil spirit to come out of the man.
Many times it had seized him, and though he
was chained hand and foot and kept under
guard, he had broken his chains and had been
driven by the demon into solitary places.

[30]Jesus asked him, "What is your name?"

"Legion," he replied, because many demons
had gone into him. [31]And they begged him
repeatedly not to order them to go into the
Abyss.

[32]A large herd of pigs was feeding there on the
hillside. The demons begged Jesus to let them
go into them, and he gave them permission.
[33]When the demons came out of the man, they
went into the pigs, and the herd rushed down
the steep bank into the lake and was drowned.

[34]When those tending the pigs saw what had
happened, they ran off and reported this in the
town and countryside, [35]and the people went out
to see what had happened. When they came to
Jesus, they found the man from whom the
demons had gone out, sitting at Jesus' feet,
dressed and in his right mind; and they were
afraid. [36]Those who had seen it told the people
how the demon-possessed man had been cured.
[37]Then all the people of the region of the
Gerasenes asked Jesus to leave them, because
they were overcome with fear. So he got into the
boat and left.

[38]The man from whom the demons had gone
out begged to go with him, but Jesus sent him
away, saying, [39]"Return home and tell how much

God has done for you." So the man went away
and told all over the town how much Jesus had
done for him.

A Dead Girl and a Sick Woman

40Now when Jesus returned, a crowd wel-
comed him, for they were all expecting him.
41Then a man named Jairus, a ruler of the syna-
gogue, came and fell at Jesus' feet, pleading with
him to come to his house 42because his only
daughter, a girl of about twelve, was dying.
As Jesus was on his way, the crowds almost
crushed him. 43And a woman was there who had
been subject to bleeding for twelve years, but
no-one could heal her. 44She came up behind
him and touched the edge of his cloak, and
immediately her bleeding stopped.
45"Who touched me?" Jesus asked.
When they all denied it, Peter said, "Master,
the people are crowding and pressing against
you."
46But Jesus said, "Someone touched me; I
know that power has gone out from me."
47Then the woman, seeing that she could not
go unnoticed, came trembling and fell at his
feet. In the presence of all the people, she told
why she had touched him and how she had been
instantly healed. 48Then he said to her, "Daugh-
ter, your faith has healed you. Go in peace."
49While Jesus was still speaking, someone
came from the house of Jairus, the synagogue
ruler. "Your daughter is dead," he said. "Don't
bother the teacher any more."
50Hearing this, Jesus said to Jairus, "Don't be
afraid; just believe, and she will be healed."
51When he arrived at the house of Jairus, he did
not let anyone go in with him except Peter, John

Two more dramatic stories of people in great distress underline the power of Jesus to deal with impossible situations.

and James, and the child's father and mother. 52 Meanwhile, all the people were wailing and mourning for her. "Stop wailing," Jesus said. "She is not dead but asleep."

53 They laughed at him, knowing that she was dead. 54 But he took her by the hand and said, "My child, get up!" 55 Her spirit returned, and at once she stood up. Then Jesus told them to give her something to eat. 56 Her parents were astonished, but he ordered them not to tell anyone what had happened.

Jesus Sends Out the Twelve

Jesus now sends out his twelve disciples to carry on his own ministry by themselves. He invests them with his own power and authority for their task.

9 When Jesus had called the Twelve together, he gave them power and authority to drive out all demons and to cure diseases, 2 and he sent them out to preach the kingdom of God and to heal the sick. 3 He told them: "Take nothing for the journey—no staff, no bag, no bread, no money, no extra tunic. 4 Whatever house you enter, stay there until you leave that town. 5 If people do not welcome you, shake the dust off your feet when you leave their town, as a testimony against them." 6 So they set out and went from village to village, preaching the gospel and healing people everywhere.

Herod, having had John the Baptist beheaded, thinks he has come back to life when news about Jesus reaches him.

7 Now Herod the tetrarch heard about all that was going on. And he was perplexed, because some were saying that John had been raised from the dead, 8 others that Elijah had appeared, and still others that one of the prophets of long ago had come back to life. 9 But Herod said, "I beheaded John. Who, then, is this I hear such things about?" And he tried to see him.

Jesus Feeds the Five Thousand

10When the apostles returned, they reported to Jesus what they had done. Then he took them with him and they withdrew by themselves to a town called Bethsaida, 11but the crowds learned about it and followed him. He welcomed them and spoke to them about the kingdom of God, and healed those who needed healing.

12Late in the afternoon the Twelve came to him and said, "Send the crowd away so they can go to the surrounding villages and countryside and find food and lodging, because we are in a remote place here."

13He replied, "You give them something to eat."

They answered, "We have only five loaves of bread and two fish—unless we go and buy food for all this crowd." 14(About five thousand men were there.)

But he said to his disciples, "Make them sit down in groups of about fifty each." 15The disciples did so, and everybody sat down. 16Taking the five loaves and the two fish and looking up to heaven, he gave thanks and broke them. Then he gave them to the disciples to set before the people. 17They all ate and were satisfied, and the disciples picked up twelve basketfuls of broken pieces that were left over.

Thousands pursue Jesus to hear his teaching and to find healing. Isolated in a remote spot without any food, they experience another sign of his power. He feeds them all with five loaves and two fish.

Peter's Confession of Christ

18Once when Jesus was praying in private and his disciples were with him, he asked them, "Who do the crowds say I am?"

19They replied, "Some say John the Baptist; others say Elijah; and still others, that one of the prophets of long ago has come back to life."

At a crucial mid-point in his public ministry, Jesus challenges the disciples to say who they think he truly is.

20"But what about you?" he asked. "Who do
you say I am?"
Peter answered, "The Christ of God."
21Jesus strictly warned them not to tell this to
anyone. 22And he said, "The Son of Man must
suffer many things and be rejected by the elders,
chief priests and teachers of the law, and he must
be killed and on the third day be raised to life."

After Peter has declared Jesus to be the Christ (or the Messiah), Jesus spells out the true cost of being one of his followers.

23Then he said to them all: "If anyone would
come after me, he must deny himself and take up
his cross daily and follow me. 24For whoever
wants to save his life will lose it, but whoever
loses his life for me will save it. 25What good is it
for a man to gain the whole world, and yet lose
or forfeit his very self? 26If anyone is ashamed of
me and my words, the Son of Man will be
ashamed of him when he comes in his glory and
in the glory of the Father and of the holy angels.
27I tell you the truth, some who are standing
here will not taste death before they see the
kingdom of God."

The Transfiguration

With only Peter, James and John around, Jesus is transfigured in brilliant light and a voice from heaven again (as at his baptism by John) declares him to be God's Son.

28About eight days after Jesus said this, he took
Peter, John and James with him and went up
onto a mountain to pray. 29As he was praying,
the appearance of his face changed, and his
clothes became as bright as a flash of lightning.
30Two men, Moses and Elijah, 31appeared in glo-
rious splendour, talking with Jesus. They spoke
about his departure, which he was about to bring
to fulfilment at Jerusalem. 32Peter and his com-
panions were very sleepy, but when they became
fully awake, they saw his glory and the two men
standing with him. 33As the men were leaving
Jesus, Peter said to him, "Master, it is good for us
to be here. Let us put up three shelters—one for

you, one for Moses and one for Elijah." (He did
not know what he was saying.)
34While he was speaking, a cloud appeared
and enveloped them, and they were afraid as
they entered the cloud. 35A voice came from the
cloud, saying, "This is my Son, whom I have
chosen; listen to him." 36When the voice had
spoken, they found that Jesus was alone. The
disciples kept this to themselves, and told no-
one at that time what they had seen.

The Healing of a Boy With an Evil Spirit

Returning to the rest of the disciples, Jesus finds them surrounded by a large crowd and at their wits' end. He shows his own power in dramatic fashion. But then he shocks and perplexes them by speaking for the first time about dark days ahead.

37The next day, when they came down from
the mountain, a large crowd met him. 38A man
in the crowd called out, "Teacher, I beg you to
look at my son, for he is my only child. 39A spirit
seizes him and he suddenly screams; it throws
him into convulsions so that he foams at the
mouth. It scarcely ever leaves him and is
destroying him. 40I begged your disciples to
drive it out, but they could not."
41"O unbelieving and perverse generation,"
Jesus replied, "how long shall I stay with you
and put up with you? Bring your son here."
42Even while the boy was coming, the demon
threw him to the ground in a convulsion. But
Jesus rebuked the evil spirit, healed the boy and
gave him back to his father. 43And they were all
amazed at the greatness of God.

While everyone was marvelling at all that
Jesus did, he said to his disciples, 44"Listen care-
fully to what I am about to tell you: The Son of
Man is going to be betrayed into the hands of
men." 45But they did not understand what this
meant. It was hidden from them, so that they did
not grasp it, and they were afraid to ask him
about it.

Who Will Be the Greatest?

Jesus talks to his disciples about true greatness.

[46]An argument started among the disciples as to which of them would be the greatest. [47]Jesus, knowing their thoughts, took a little child and made him stand beside him. [48]Then he said to them, "Whoever welcomes this little child in my name welcomes me; and whoever welcomes me welcomes the one who sent me. For he who is least among you all—he is the greatest."

[49]"Master," said John, "we saw a man driving out demons in your name and we tried to stop him, because he is not one of us."

[50]"Do not stop him," Jesus said, "for whoever is not against you is for you."

Samaritan Opposition

Jesus rebukes his disciples for their racial prejudice against the Samaritans.

[51]As the time approached for him to be taken up to heaven, Jesus resolutely set out for Jerusalem. [52]And he sent messengers on ahead, who went into a Samaritan village to get things ready for him; [53]but the people there did not welcome him, because he was heading for Jerusalem. [54]When the disciples James and John saw this, they asked, "Lord, do you want us to call fire down from heaven to destroy them?" [55]But Jesus turned and rebuked them, [56]and they went to another village.

The Cost of Following Jesus

Jesus again spells out to his disciples that he must come first in their lives.

[57]As they were walking along the road, a man said to him, "I will follow you wherever you go."

[58]Jesus replied, "Foxes have holes and birds of the air have nests, but the Son of Man has nowhere to lay his head."

[59]He said to another man, "Follow me."

But the man replied, "Lord, first let me go and bury my father."

60Jesus said to him, "Let the dead bury their own dead, but you go and proclaim the kingdom of God."

61Still another said, "I will follow you, Lord; but first let me go back and say good-bye to my family."

62Jesus replied, "No-one who puts his hand to the plough and looks back is fit for service in the kingdom of God."

Jesus Sends Out the Seventy-two

10 After this the Lord appointed seventy-two others and sent them two by two ahead of him to every town and place where he was about to go. 2He told them, "The harvest is plentiful, but the workers are few. Ask the Lord of the harvest, therefore, to send out workers into his harvest field. 3Go! I am sending you out like lambs among wolves. 4Do not take a purse or bag or sandals; and do not greet anyone on the road.

A further seventy-two followers are sent out by Jesus to carry on his ministry with his authority and facing the same dangers.

5"When you enter a house, first say, 'Peace to this house.' 6If a man of peace is there, your peace will rest on him; if not, it will return to you. 7Stay in that house, eating and drinking whatever they give you, for the worker deserves his wages. Do not move around from house to house.

8"When you enter a town and are welcomed, eat what is set before you. 9Heal the sick who are there and tell them, 'The kingdom of God is near you.' 10But when you enter a town and are not welcomed, go into its streets and say 11'Even the dust of your town that sticks to our feet we wipe off against you. Yet be sure of this: The

kingdom of God is near.' 12I tell you, it will be
more bearable on that day for Sodom than for
that town.

13"Woe to you, Korazin! Woe to you, Beth-
saida! For if the miracles that were performed in
you had been performed in Tyre and Sidon, they
would have repented long ago, sitting in sack-
cloth and ashes. 14But it will be more bearable
for Tyre and Sidon at the judgment than for you.
15And you, Capernaum, will you be lifted up to
the skies? No, you will go down to the depths.

16"He who listens to you listens to me; he who
rejects you rejects me; but he who rejects me
rejects him who sent me."

When the seventy-two return in a buoyant mood, Jesus makes them concentrate, not on dramatic results, but on their security as children of God.

17The seventy-two returned with joy and said,
"Lord, even the demons submit to us in your
name."

18He replied, "I saw Satan fall like lightning
from heaven. 19I have given you authority to
trample on snakes and scorpions and to over-
come all the power of the enemy; nothing will
harm you. 20However, do not rejoice that the
spirits submit to you, but rejoice that your
names are written in heaven."

21At that time Jesus, full of joy through the
Holy Spirit, said, "I praise you, Father, Lord of
heaven and earth, because you have hidden
these things from the wise and learned, and
revealed them to little children. Yes, Father, for
this was your good pleasure.

22"All things have been committed to me by
my Father. No-one knows who the Son is except
the Father, and no-one knows who the Father is
except the Son and those to whom the Son
chooses to reveal him."

23Then he turned to his disciples and said pri-
vately, "Blessed are the eyes that see what you

see. 24For I tell you that many prophets and
kings wanted to see what you see but did not see
it, and to hear what you hear but did not hear it."

The Parable of the Good Samaritan

25On one occasion an expert in the law stood
up to test Jesus. "Teacher," he asked, "what must
I do to inherit eternal life?"
26"What is written in the Law?" he replied.
"How do you read it?"
27He answered: "'Love the Lord your God
with all your heart and with all your soul and
with all your strength and with all your mind';
and, 'Love your neighbour as yourself.'"
28"You have answered correctly," Jesus replied.
"Do this and you will live."
29But he wanted to justify himself, so he asked
Jesus, "And who is my neighbour?"
30In reply Jesus said: "A man was going down
from Jerusalem to Jericho, when he fell into the
hands of robbers. They stripped him of his
clothes, beat him and went away, leaving him
half-dead. 31A priest happened to be going down
the same road, and when he saw the man, he
passed by on the other side. 32So too, a Levite,
when he came to the place and saw him, passed
by on the other side. 33But a Samaritan, as he
travelled, came where the man was; and when he
saw him, he took pity on him. 34He went to him
and bandaged his wounds, pouring on oil and
wine. Then he put the man on his own donkey,
brought him to an inn and took care of him.
35The next day he took out two silver coins and
gave them to the innkeeper. 'Look after him,' he
said, 'and when I return, I will reimburse you for
any extra expense you may have.'
36"Which of these three do you think was a

Challenged by a lawyer about what really matters to God, Jesus makes the man face up to the personal implications of the commandment to love your neighbour as yourself. He tells a story which calls for practical love towards anyone in need who crosses our path.

neighbour to the man who fell into the hands of
robbers?"
37The expert in the law replied, "The one who
had mercy on him."
Jesus told him, "Go and do likewise."

At the Home of Martha and Mary

Jesus gently confronts a busy activist with the priority of taking time for listening to God.

38As Jesus and his disciples were on their way,
he came to a village where a woman named
Martha opened her home to him. 39She had a
sister called Mary, who sat at the Lord's feet lis-
tening to what he said. 40But Martha was dis-
tracted by all the preparations that had to be
made. She came to him and asked, "Lord, don't
you care that my sister has left me to do the work
by myself? Tell her to help me!"
41"Martha, Martha," the Lord answered, "you
are worried and upset about many things, 42but
only one thing is needed. Mary has chosen what
is better, and it will not be taken away from her."

Jesus' Teaching on Prayer

Jesus inspires his disciples to pray by his example and his teaching.

11 One day Jesus was praying in a certain
place. When he finished, one of his dis-
ciples said to him, "Lord, teach us to pray, just as
John taught his disciples."
2He said to them, "When you pray, say:

"'Father,
hallowed be your name,
your kingdom come.
3Give us each day our daily bread.
4Forgive us our sins,
for we also forgive everyone who sins
against us.
And lead us not into temptation.'"

5Then he said to them, "Suppose one of you
has a friend, and he goes to him at midnight and
says, 'Friend, lend me three loaves of bread,
6because a friend of mine on a journey has come
to me, and I have nothing to set before him.'
7"Then the one inside answers, 'Don't bother
me. The door is already locked, and my children
are with me in bed. I can't get up and give you
anything.' 8I tell you, though he will not get up
and give him the bread because he is his friend,
yet because of the man's boldness he will get up
and give him as much as he needs.
9"So I say to you: Ask and it will be given to
you; seek and you will find; knock and the door
will be opened to you. 10For everyone who asks
receives; he who seeks finds; and to him who
knocks, the door will be opened.
11"Which of you fathers, if your son asks for a
fish, will give him a snake instead? 12Or if he asks
for an egg, will give him a scorpion? 13If you
then, though you are evil, know how to give
good gifts to your children, how much more will
your Father in heaven give the Holy Spirit to
those who ask him!"

Jesus and Beelzebub

14Jesus was driving out a demon that was
mute. When the demon left, the man who had
been mute spoke, and the crowd was amazed.
15But some of them said, "By Beelzebub, the
prince of demons, he is driving out demons."
16Others tested him by asking for a sign from
heaven.
17Jesus knew their thoughts and said to them:
"Any kingdom divided against itself will be
ruined, and a house divided against itself will

Jesus again demonstrates his power over demonic forces. He explains the way this power expresses the presence of God's kingdom.

fall. 18If Satan is divided against himself, how can his kingdom stand? I say this because you claim that I drive out demons by Beelzebub. 19Now if I drive out demons by Beelzebub, by whom do your followers drive them out? So then, they will be your judges. 20But if I drive out demons by the finger of God, then the kingdom of God has come to you.

21"When a strong man, fully armed, guards his own house, his possessions are safe. 22But when someone stronger attacks and overpowers him, he takes away the armour in which the man trusted and divides up the spoils.

23"He who is not with me is against me, and he who does not gather with me, scatters.

24"When an evil spirit comes out of a man, it goes through arid places seeking rest and does not find it. Then it says, 'I will return to the house I left.' 25When it arrives, it finds the house swept clean and put in order. 26Then it goes and takes seven other spirits more wicked than itself, and they go in and live there. And the final condition of that man is worse than the first."

27As Jesus was saying these things, a woman in the crowd called out, "Blessed is the mother who gave you birth and nursed you."

28He replied, "Blessed rather are those who hear the word of God and obey it."

The Sign of Jonah

As the crowds continue to grow and demand more miracles, Jesus stresses that it is his message which is more important.

29As the crowds increased, Jesus said, "This is a wicked generation. It asks for a miraculous sign, but none will be given it except the sign of Jonah. 30For as Jonah was a sign to the Ninevites, so also will the Son of Man be to this generation. 31The Queen of the South will rise at the judgment with the men of this generation

and condemn them; for she came from the ends
of the earth to listen to Solomon's wisdom, and
now one greater than Solomon is here. 32The
men of Nineveh will stand up at the judgment
with this generation and condemn it; for they
repented at the preaching of Jonah, and now
one greater than Jonah is here.

The Lamp of the Body

33"No-one lights a lamp and puts it in a place
where it will be hidden, or under a bowl. Instead
he puts it on its stand, so that those who come in
may see the light. 34Your eye is the lamp of your
body. When your eyes are good, your whole body
also is full of light. But when they are bad, your
body also is full of darkness. 35See to it, then, that
the light within you is not darkness. 36Therefore,
if your whole body is full of light, and no part of it
dark, it will be completely lighted, as when the
light of a lamp shines on you."

Jesus also stresses that a key part in our lives is the way we use our eyes.

Six Woes

37When Jesus had finished speaking, a Phar-
isee invited him to eat with him; so he went in
and reclined at the table. 38But the Pharisee,
noticing that Jesus did not first wash before the
meal, was surprised.

39Then the Lord said to him, "Now then, you
Pharisees clean the outside of the cup and dish,
but inside you are full of greed and wickedness.
40You foolish people! Did not the one who made
the outside make the inside also? 41But give
what is inside [the dish] to the poor, and every-
thing will be clean for you.

42"Woe to you Pharisees, because you give
God a tenth of your mint, rue and all other kinds

He warns the Pharisees about the shallow hypocrisy of their emphasis on externals, to the neglect of justice and compassion.

of garden herbs, but you neglect justice and the love of God. You should have practised the latter without leaving the former undone.

43"Woe to you Pharisees, because you love the most important seats in the synagogues and greetings in the market-places.

44"Woe to you, because you are like unmarked graves, which men walk over without knowing it."

Jesus charges the teachers of the law with laying heavy burdens on the people. They, as well as the Pharisees, are incensed and step up their opposition.

45One of the experts in the law answered him, "Teacher, when you say these things, you insult us also."

46Jesus replied, "And you experts in the law, woe to you, because you load people down with burdens they can hardly carry, and you yourselves will not lift one finger to help them.

47"Woe to you, because you build tombs for
the prophets, and it was your forefathers who
killed them. 48So you testify that you approve of
what your forefathers did; they killed the
prophets, and you build their tombs. 49Because
of this, God in his wisdom said, 'I will send them
prophets and apostles, some of whom they will
kill and others they will persecute.' 50Therefore
this generation will be held responsible for the
blood of all the prophets that has been shed
since the beginning of the world, 51from the
blood of Abel to the blood of Zechariah, who
was killed between the altar and the sanctuary.
Yes, I tell you, this generation will be held
responsible for it all.

52"Woe to you experts in the law, because you have taken away the key to knowledge. You yourselves have not entered, and you have hindered those who were entering."

53When Jesus left there, the Pharisees and the teachers of the law began to oppose him fiercely

and to besiege him with questions, 54waiting to
catch him in something he might say.

Warnings and Encouragements

12 Meanwhile, when a crowd of many thou
sands had gathered, so that they were
trampling on one another, Jesus began to speak
first to his disciples, saying: "Be on your guard
against the yeast of the Pharisees, which is
hypocrisy. 2There is nothing concealed that will
not be disclosed, or hidden that will not be made
known. 3What you have said in the dark will be
heard in the daylight, and what you have whis-
pered in the ear in the inner rooms will be pro-
claimed from the roofs.

In the increasingly hostile climate, Jesus reassures his disciples about the power of God to provide everything they will need.

4"I tell you, my friends, do not be afraid of
those who kill the body and after that can do no
more. 5But I will show you whom you should
fear: Fear him who, after the killing of the body,
has power to throw you into hell. Yes, I tell you,
fear him. 6Are not five sparrows sold for two
pennies? Yet not one of them is forgotten by
God. 7Indeed, the very hairs of your head are all
numbered. Don't be afraid; you are worth more
than many sparrows.

8"I tell you, whoever acknowledges me before
men, the Son of Man will also acknowledge him
before the angels of God. 9But he who disowns
me before men will be disowned before the
angels of God. 10And everyone who speaks a
word against the Son of Man will be forgiven,
but anyone who blasphemes against the Holy
Spirit will not be forgiven.

11"When you are brought before synagogues,
rulers and authorities, do not worry about how
you will defend yourselves or what you will say,

12for the Holy Spirit will teach you at that time
what you should say."

The Parable of the Rich Fool

Jesus warns everyone about the dangers of greed in all its forms.

13Someone in the crowd said to him, "Teacher,
tell my brother to divide the inheritance with
me."
14Jesus replied, "Man, who appointed me a
judge or an arbiter between you?" 15Then he
said to them, "Watch out! Be on your guard
against all kinds of greed; a man's life does not
consist in the abundance of his possessions."
16And he told them this parable: "The ground
of a certain rich man produced a good crop.
17He thought to himself, 'What shall I do? I have
no place to store my crops.'
18"Then he said, 'This is what I'll do. I will tear
down my barns and build bigger ones, and there
I will store all my grain and my goods. 19And I'll
say to myself, "You have plenty of good things
laid up for many years. Take life easy; eat, drink
and be merry."'
20"But God said to him, 'You fool! This very
night your life will be demanded from you.
Then who will get what you have prepared for
yourself?'
21"This is how it will be with anyone who
stores up things for himself but is not rich
towards God."

Do Not Worry

Trusting God to provide is the antidote to the anxiety caused by materialism.

22Then Jesus said to his disciples: "Therefore I
tell you, do not worry about your life, what you
will eat; or about your body, what you will wear.
23Life is more than food, and the body more
than clothes. 24Consider the ravens: They do
not sow or reap, they have no storeroom or barn;

yet God feeds them. And how much more valu-
able you are than birds! [25]Who of you by worry-
ing can add a single hour to his life? [26]Since you
cannot do this very little thing, why do you
worry about the rest?

[27]"Consider how the lilies grow. They do not
labour or spin. Yet I tell you, not even Solomon
in all his splendour was dressed like one of these.
[28]If that is how God clothes the grass of the
field, which is here today, and tomorrow is
thrown into the fire, how much more will he
clothe you, O you of little faith! [29]And do not set
your heart on what you will eat or drink; do not
worry about it. [30]For the pagan world runs after
all such things, and your Father knows that you
need them. [31]But seek his kingdom, and these
things will be given to you as well.

[32]"Do not be afraid, little flock, for your
Father has been pleased to give you the king-
dom. [33]Sell your possessions and give to the
poor. Provide purses for yourselves that will not
wear out, a treasure in heaven that will not be
exhausted, where no thief comes near and no
moth destroys. [34]For where your treasure is,
there your heart will be also.

Watchfulness

[35]"Be dressed ready for service and keep your
lamps burning, [36]like men waiting for their mas-
ter to return from a wedding banquet, so that
when he comes and knocks they can immediate-
ly open the door for him. [37]It will be good for
those servants whose master finds them watch-
ing when he comes. I tell you the truth, he will
dress himself to serve, will have them recline at
the table and will come and wait on them. [38]It
will be good for those servants whose master

Instead of living for today or tomorrow, live in the light of eternity, especially being on the alert for the day of reckoning, when our lives will be scrutinised by God.

finds them ready, even if he comes in the second or third watch of the night. 39But understand this: If the owner of the house had known at what hour the thief was coming, he would not have let his house be broken into. 40You also must be ready, because the Son of Man will come at an hour when you do not expect him."

41Peter asked, "Lord, are you telling this parable to us, or to everyone?"

42The Lord answered, "Who then is the faithful and wise manager, whom the master puts in charge of his servants to give them their food allowance at the proper time? 43It will be good for that servant whom the master finds doing so when he returns. 44I tell you the truth, he will put him in charge of all his possessions. 45But suppose the servant says to himself, 'My master is taking a long time in coming,' and he then begins to beat the menservants and maidservants and to eat and drink and get drunk. 46The master of that servant will come on a day when he does not expect him and at an hour he is not aware of. He will cut him to pieces and assign him a place with the unbelievers.

47"That servant who knows his master's will and does not get ready or does not do what his master wants will be beaten with many blows. 48But the one who does not know and does things deserving punishment will be beaten with few blows. From everyone who has been given much, much will be demanded; and from the one who has been entrusted with much, much more will be asked.

Not Peace but Division

To be a follower of Jesus will bring division in families.

49"I have come to bring fire on the earth, and how I wish it were already kindled! 50But I have a baptism to undergo, and how distressed I am until it is completed! 51 Do you think I came to bring peace on earth? No, I tell you, but division. 52 From now on there will be five in one family divided against each other, three against two and two against three. 53 They will be divided, father against son and son against father, mother against daughter and daughter against mother, mother-in-law against daughter-in-law and daughter-in-law against mother-in-law."

Interpreting the Times

54 He said to the crowd: "When you see a cloud rising in the west, immediately you say, 'It's going to rain,' and it does. 55 And when the south wind blows, you say, 'It's going to be hot,' and it is. 56 Hypocrites! You know how to interpret the appearance of the earth and the sky. How is it that you don't know how to interpret this present time?

If you read the signs correctly, you will take sensible decisions about what really matters in your daily lives.

57 "Why don't you judge for yourselves what is right? 58 As you are going with your adversary to the magistrate, try hard to be reconciled to him on the way, or he may drag you off to the judge, and the judge turn you over to the officer, and the officer throw you into prison. 59 I tell you, you will not get out until you have paid the last penny."

Repent or Perish

13 Now there were some present at that time who told Jesus about the Galileans whose blood Pilate had mixed with their sacrifices. 2 Jesus answered, "Do you think that these Galileans were worse sinners than all the other Galileans because they suffered this way? 3 I tell

Disasters and tragedies should alert us to keep a right relationship with God.

you, no! But unless you repent, you too will all
perish. 4Or those eighteen who died when the
tower in Siloam fell on them—do you think they
were more guilty than all the others living in
Jerusalem? 5I tell you, no! But unless you repent,
you too will all perish."

6Then he told this parable: "A man had a fig-
tree, planted in his vineyard, and he went to look
for fruit on it, but did not find any. 7So he said to
the man who took care of the vineyard, 'For
three years now I've been coming to look for
fruit on this fig-tree and haven't found any. Cut
it down! Why should it use up the soil?'

8"'Sir,' the man replied, 'leave it alone for one
more year, and I'll dig round it and fertilise it. 9If
it bears fruit next year, fine! If not, then cut it
down.'"

A Crippled Woman Healed on the Sabbath

Another act of healing on a Sabbath day provokes more hostility from the religious authorities.

10On a Sabbath Jesus was teaching in one of
the synagogues, 11and a woman was there who
had been crippled by a spirit for eighteen years.
She was bent over and could not straighten up at
all. 12When Jesus saw her, he called her forward
and said to her, "Woman, you are set free from
your infirmity." 13Then he put his hands on her,
and immediately she straightened up and
praised God.

14Indignant because Jesus had healed on the
Sabbath, the synagogue ruler said to the people,
"There are six days for work. So come and be
healed on those days, not on the Sabbath."

15The Lord answered him, "You hypocrites!
Doesn't each of you on the Sabbath untie his ox
or donkey from the stall and lead it out to give it
water? 16Then should not this woman, a daugh-
ter of Abraham, whom Satan has kept bound for

eighteen long years, be set free on the Sabbath day from what bound her?"

17When he said this, all his opponents were humiliated, but the people were delighted with all the wonderful things he was doing.

The Parables of the Mustard Seed and the Yeast

18Then Jesus asked, "What is the kingdom of
God like? What shall I compare it to? 19It is like
a mustard seed, which a man took and planted in his garden. It grew and became a tree, and the birds of the air perched in its branches."

The kingdom of God grows from small beginnings and in hidden ways.

20Again he asked, "What shall I compare the
kingdom of God to? 21It is like yeast that a
woman took and mixed into a large amount of flour until it worked all through the dough."

The Narrow Door

22Then Jesus went through the towns and villages, teaching as he made his way to Jerusalem.
23Someone asked him, "Lord, are only a few people going to be saved?"

There is more to the teaching of Jesus than mere listening: action is required now.

He said to them, 24"Make every effort to enter
through the narrow door, because many, I tell you, will try to enter and will not be able to.
25Once the owner of the house gets up and closes the door, you will stand outside knocking and pleading, 'Sir, open the door for us.'

"But he will answer, 'I don't know you or where you come from.'

26"Then you will say, 'We ate and drank with you, and you taught in our streets.'

27"But he will reply, 'I don't know you or where you come from. Away from me, all you evildoers!'

[28]"There will be weeping there, and gnashing of teeth, when you see Abraham, Isaac and Jacob and all the prophets in the kingdom of God, but you yourselves thrown out. [29]People will come from east and west and north and south, and will take their places at the feast in the kingdom of God. [30]Indeed there are those who are last who will be first, and first who will be last."

Jesus' Sorrow for Jerusalem

Jesus' life is now under serious threat. He is more concerned for what this hostility indicates about the spiritual state of the city.

[31]At that time some Pharisees came to Jesus and said to him, "Leave this place and go somewhere else. Herod wants to kill you."

[32]He replied, "Go tell that fox, 'I will drive out demons and heal people today and tomorrow, and on the third day I will reach my goal.' [33]In any case, I must keep going today and tomorrow and the next day—for surely no prophet can die outside Jerusalem!

[34]"O Jerusalem, Jerusalem, you who kill the prophets and stone those sent to you, how often I have longed to gather your children together, as a hen gathers her chicks under her wings, but you were not willing! [35]Look, your house is left to you desolate. I tell you, you will not see me again until you say, 'Blessed is he who comes in the name of the Lord.'"

Jesus at a Pharisee's House

Still accepting the hospitality of hostile opponents determined to trap him, Jesus talks about the kind of socialising and hospitality which he recommends.

14 One Sabbath, when Jesus went to eat in the house of a prominent Pharisee, he was being carefully watched. [2]There in front of him was a man suffering from dropsy. [3]Jesus asked the Pharisees and experts in the law, "Is it lawful to heal on the Sabbath or not?" [4]But they remained silent. So taking hold of the man, he

healed him and sent him away.
5Then he asked them, "If one of you has a son
or an ox that falls into a well on the Sabbath day,
will you not immediately pull him out?" 6And
they had nothing to say.
7When he noticed how the guests picked the
places of honour at the table, he told them this
parable: 8"When someone invites you to a wed-
ding feast, do not take the place of honour, for a
person more distinguished than you may have
been invited. 9If so, the host who invited both of
you will come and say to you, 'Give this man
your seat.' Then, humiliated, you will have to
take the least important place. 10But when you
are invited, take the lowest place, so that when
your host comes, he will say to you, 'Friend,
move up to a better place.' Then you will be
honoured in the presence of all your fellow
guests. 11For everyone who exalts himself will
be humbled, and he who humbles himself will
be exalted."
12Then Jesus said to his host, "When you give
a luncheon or dinner, do not invite your friends,
your brothers or relatives, or your rich neigh-
bours; if you do, they may invite you back and so
you will be repaid. 13But when you give a ban-
quet, invite the poor, the crippled, the lame, the
blind, 14and you will be blessed. Although they
cannot repay you, you will be repaid at the res-
urrection of the righteous."

The Parable of the Great Banquet

15When one of those at the table with him
heard this, he said to Jesus, "Blessed is the man
who will eat at the feast in the kingdom of God."
16Jesus replied: "A certain man was preparing
a great banquet and invited many guests. 17At

Still sitting around his host's dinner-table, Jesus talks about the greatest banquet of all – in the kingdom of God.

the time of the banquet he sent his servant to tell those who had been invited, 'Come, for everything is now ready.'

18"But they all alike began to make excuses. The first said, 'I have just bought a field, and I must go and see it. Please excuse me.'

19"Another said, 'I have just bought five yoke of oxen, and I'm on my way to try them out. Please excuse me.'

20"Still another said, 'I have just got married, so I can't come.'

21"The servant came back and reported this to his master. Then the owner of the house became angry and ordered his servant, 'Go out quickly into the streets and alleys of the town and bring in the poor, the crippled, the blind and the lame.'

22" 'Sir,' the servant said, 'what you ordered has been done, but there is still room.'

23"Then the master told his servant, 'Go out to the roads and country lanes and make them come in, so that my house will be full. 24I tell you, not one of those men who were invited will get a taste of my banquet.' "

The Cost of Being a Disciple

Again Jesus tells the large crowds following him about the cost of being his disciple.

25Large crowds were travelling with Jesus, and turning to them he said: 26"If anyone comes to me and does not hate his father and mother, his wife and children, his brothers and sisters—yes, even his own life—he cannot be my disciple. 27And anyone who does not carry his cross and follow me cannot be my disciple.

28"Suppose one of you wants to build a tower. Will he not first sit down and estimate the cost to see if he has enough money to complete it? 29For if he lays the foundation and is not able to finish it, everyone who sees it will ridicule him, 30 saying, 'This fellow began to build and was not able to finish.'

31 "Or suppose a king is about to go to war against another king. Will he not first sit down and consider whether he is able with ten thousand men to oppose the one coming against him with twenty thousand? 32 If he is not able, he will send a delegation while the other is still a long way off and will ask for terms of peace. 33 In the same way, any of you who does not give up everything he has cannot be my disciple.

34 "Salt is good, but if it loses its saltiness, how can it be made salty again? 35 It is fit neither for the soil nor for the manure heap; it is thrown out.

"He who has ears to hear, let him hear."

The Parable of the Lost Sheep

15 Now the tax collectors and "sinners" were all gathering round to hear him. 2 But the Pharisees and the teachers of the law muttered, "This man welcomes sinners, and eats with them."

While the Pharisees criticise Jesus for consorting with those they regard as the lowest of the low, he tells three vivid stories to highlight God's compassionate searching for those who are lost.

3 Then Jesus told them this parable: 4 "Suppose one of you has a hundred sheep and loses one of them. Does he not leave the ninety-nine in the open country and go after the lost sheep until he finds it? 5 And when he finds it, he joyfully puts it on his shoulders 6 and goes home. Then he calls his friends and neighbours together and says, 'Rejoice with me; I have found my lost sheep.' 7 I tell you that in the same way there will be more rejoicing in heaven over one sinner who repents than over ninety-nine righteous persons who do not need to repent.

The Parable of the Lost Coin

8“Or suppose a woman has ten silver coins and loses one. Does she not light a lamp, sweep the house and search carefully until she finds it? 9And when she finds it, she calls her friends and neighbours together and says, ‘Rejoice with me; I have found my lost coin.’ 10In the same way, I tell you, there is rejoicing in the presence of the angels of God over one sinner who repents.”

The Parable of the Lost Son

This third story underlines God's equally undying love, both for the wild and for the dutiful.

11Jesus continued: “There was a man who had two sons. 12The younger one said to his father, ‘Father, give me my share of the estate.’ So he divided his property between them.

13“Not long after that, the younger son got together all he had, set off for a distant country and there squandered his wealth in wild living. 14After he had spent everything, there was a severe famine in that whole country, and he began to be in need. 15So he went and hired himself out to a citizen of that country, who sent him to his fields to feed pigs. 16He longed to fill his stomach with the pods that the pigs were eating, but no-one gave him anything.

17“When he came to his senses, he said, ‘How many of my father's hired men have food to spare, and here I am starving to death! 18I will set out and go back to my father and say to him: Father, I have sinned against heaven and against you. 19I am no longer worthy to be called your son; make me like one of your hired men.’ 20So he got up and went to his father.

“But while he was still a long way off, his father saw him and was filled with compassion for him;

he ran to his son, threw his arms around him and kissed him.

21“The son said to him, ‘Father, I have sinned against heaven and against you. I am no longer worthy to be called your son.’

22“But the father said to his servants, ‘Quick! Bring the best robe and put it on him. Put a ring on his finger and sandals on his feet. 23Bring the fattened calf and kill it. Let’s have a feast and celebrate. 24For this son of mine was dead and is alive again; he was lost and is found.’ So they began to celebrate.

25“Meanwhile, the older son was in the field. When he came near the house, he heard music and dancing. 26So he called one of the servants and asked him what was going on. 27‘Your brother has come,’ he replied, ‘and your father has killed the fattened calf because he has him back safe and sound.’

28“The older brother became angry and refused to go in. So his father went out and pleaded with him. 29But hc answered his tather, ‘Look! All these years I’ve been slaving for you and never disobeyed your orders. Yet you never gave me even a young goat so I could celebrate with my friends. 30But when this son of yours who has squandered your property with prostitutes comes home, you kill the fattened calf for him!’

31“‘My son,’ the father said, ‘you are always with me, and everything I have is yours. 32But we had to celebrate and be glad, because this brother of yours was dead and is alive again; he was lost and is found.’”

The Parable of the Shrewd Manager

Men of the world often use wealth shrewdly. Jesus warns against the inherent power which wealth exercises over people, calling for honesty and integrity. The Pharisees, who are in the grip of covetousness, sneer at Jesus.

16 Jesus told his disciples: "There was a rich man whose manager was accused of wasting his possessions. [2]So he called him in and asked him, 'What is this I hear about you? Give an account of your management, because you cannot be manager any longer.'

[3]"The manager said to himself, 'What shall I do now? My master is taking away my job. I'm not strong enough to dig, and I'm ashamed to beg—[4]I know what I'll do so that, when I lose my job here, people will welcome me into their houses.'

[5]"So he called in each one of his master's debtors. He asked the first, 'How much do you owe my master?'

[6]" 'Eight hundred gallons of olive oil,' he replied.

"The manager told him, 'Take your bill, sit down quickly, and make it four hundred.'

[7]"Then he asked the second, 'And how much do you owe?'

" 'A thousand bushels of wheat,' he replied.

"He told him, 'Take your bill and make it eight hundred.'

[8]"The master commended the dishonest manager because he had acted shrewdly. For the people of this world are more shrewd in dealing with their own kind than are the people of the light. [9]I tell you, use worldly wealth to gain friends for yourselves, so that when it is gone, you will be welcomed into eternal dwellings.

[10]"Whoever can be trusted with very little can also be trusted with much, and whoever is dishonest with very little will also be dishonest with much. [11]So if you have not been trustworthy in handling worldly wealth, who will trust you with

true riches? 12And if you have not been trust-
worthy with someone else's property, who will
give you property of your own?
13"No servant can serve two masters. Either
he will hate the one and love the other, or he will
be devoted to the one and despise the other. You
cannot serve both God and Money."
14The Pharisees, who loved money, heard all
this and were sneering at Jesus. 15He said to
them, "You are the ones who justify yourselves
in the eyes of men, but God knows your hearts.
What is highly valued among men is detestable
in God's sight.

Additional Teachings

16"The Law and the Prophets were pro-
claimed until John. Since that time, the good
news of the kingdom of God is being preached,
and everyone is forcing his way into it. 17It is
easier for heaven and earth to disappear than for
the least stroke of a pen to drop out of the Law.

Jesus emphasises the permanent relevance and authority of the Law and the Prophets.

18"Anyone who divorces his wife and marries
another woman commits adultery, and the man
who marries a divorced woman commits adul-
tery.

The Rich Man and Lazarus

19"There was a rich man who was dressed in
purple and fine linen and lived in luxury every
day. 20At his gate was laid a beggar named
Lazarus, covered with sores 21and longing to eat
what fell from the rich man's table. Even the
dogs came and licked his sores.
22"The time came when the beggar died and
the angels carried him to Abraham's side. The
rich man also died and was buried. 23In hell,

Jesus describes the callous indifference which often goes with a luxurious lifestyle. This has appalling consequences into eternity.

where he was in torment, he looked up and saw
Abraham far away, with Lazarus by his side. 24So
he called to him, 'Father Abraham, have pity on
me and send Lazarus to dip the tip of his finger
in water and cool my tongue, because I am in
agony in this fire.'
25"But Abraham replied, 'Son, remember that
in your lifetime you received your good things,
while Lazarus received bad things, but now he is
comforted here and you are in agony. 26And
besides all this, between us and you a great
chasm has been fixed, so that those who want to
go from here to you cannot, nor can anyone
cross over from there to us.'
27"He answered, 'Then I beg you, father, send
Lazarus to my father's house, 28for I have five
brothers. Let him warn them, so that they will
not also come to this place of torment.'
29"Abraham replied, 'They have Moses and
the Prophets; let them listen to them.'
30" 'No, father Abraham,' he said, 'but if some-
one from the dead goes to them, they will
repent.'
31"He said to him, 'If they do not listen to
Moses and the Prophets, they will not be con-
vinced even if someone rises from the dead.' "

Sin, Faith, Duty

Further insights into the responsibilities and duties of being disciples of Jesus.

17 Jesus said to his disciples: "Things that
cause people to sin are bound to come,
but woe to that person through whom they
come. 2It would be better for him to be thrown
into the sea with a millstone tied round his neck
than for him to cause one of these little ones to
sin. 3So watch yourselves.
"If your brother sins, rebuke him, and if he

repents, forgive him. [4]If he sins against you seven times in a day, and seven times comes back to you and says, 'I repent,' forgive him."

[5]The apostles said to the Lord, "Increase our faith!"

[6]He replied, "If you have faith as small as a mustard seed, you can say to this mulberry tree, 'Be uprooted and planted in the sea,' and it will obey you.

[7]"Suppose one of you had a servant ploughing or looking after the sheep. Would he say to the servant when he comes in from the field, 'Come along now and sit down to eat'? [8]Would he not rather say, 'Prepare my supper, get yourself ready and wait on me while I eat and drink; after that you may eat and drink'? [9]Would he thank the servant because he did what he was told to do? [10]So you also, when you have done everything you were told to do, should say, 'We are unworthy servants; we have only done our duty.'"

Ten Healed of Leprosy

[11]Now on his way to Jerusalem, Jesus travelled along the border between Samaria and Galilee. [12]As he was going into a village, ten men who had leprosy met him. They stood at a distance [13]and called out in a loud voice, "Jesus, Master, have pity on us!"

Jesus heals ten lepers. Only one returns to say thank you. Jesus underlines the link between gratitude, faith and well-being.

[14]When he saw them, he said, "Go, show yourselves to the priests." And as they went, they were cleansed.

[15]One of them, when he saw he was healed, came back, praising God in a loud voice. [16]He threw himself at Jesus' feet and thanked him—and he was a Samaritan.

[17]Jesus asked, "Were not all ten cleansed?

Where are the other nine? 18Was no-one found
to return and give praise to God except this for-
eigner?" 19Then he said to him, "Rise and go;
your faith has made you well."

The Coming of the Kingdom of God

Returning to the theme of God's kingdom, now and in the future, Jesus looks forward to the day when he, the Son of Man, will be fully vindicated. Now he is heading for suffering and rejection.

20Once, having been asked by the Pharisees
when the kingdom of God would come, Jesus
replied, "The kingdom of God does not come
with your careful observation, 21nor will people
say, 'Here it is,' or 'There it is,' because the king-
dom of God is within you."

22Then he said to his disciples, "The time is
coming when you will long to see one of the days
of the Son of Man, but you will not see it. 23Men
will tell you, 'There he is!' or 'Here he is!' Do
not go running off after them. 24For the Son of
Man in his day will be like the lightning, which
flashes and lights up the sky from one end to the
other. 25But first he must suffer many things and
be rejected by this generation.

26"Just as it was in the days of Noah, so also will
it be in the days of the Son of Man. 27People
were eating, drinking, marrying and being given
in marriage up to the day Noah entered the ark.
Then the flood came and destroyed them all.

28"It was the same in the days of Lot. People
were eating and drinking, buying and selling,
planting and building. 29But the day Lot left
Sodom, fire and sulphur rained down from
heaven and destroyed them all.

30"It will be just like this on the day the Son of
Man is revealed. 31On that day no-one who is on
the roof of his house, with his goods inside,
should go down to get them. Likewise, no-one
in the field should go back for anything.
32Remember Lot's wife! 33Whoever tries to keep

his life will lose it, and whoever loses his life will
preserve it. 34I tell you, on that night two people
will be in one bed; one will be taken and the
other left. 35Two women will be grinding grain
together; one will be taken and the other left."
37"Where, Lord?" they asked.

He replied, "Where there is a dead body, there the vultures will gather."

The Parable of the Persistent Widow

18 Then Jesus told his disciples a parable to
show them that they should always pray
and not give up. 2He said: "In a certain town
there was a judge who neither feared God nor
cared about men. 3And there was a widow in that
town who kept coming to him with the plea,
'Grant me justice against my adversary.'
4"For some time he refused. But finally he said
to himself, 'Even though I don't fear God or
care about men, 5yet because this widow keeps
bothering me, I will see that she gets justice, so
that she won't eventually wear me out with her
coming!'"
6And the Lord said, "Listen to what the unjust
judge says. 7And will not God bring about jus-
tice for his chosen ones, who cry out to him day
and night? Will he keep putting them off? 8I tell
you, he will see that they get justice, and quickly.
However, when the Son of Man comes, will he
find faith on the earth?"

Jesus tells his disciples to keep on praying and to keep on believing.

The Parable of the Pharisee and the Tax Collector

9To some who were confident of their own
righteousness and looked down on everybody

Jesus here directly contrasts representatives of the two groupings around ➤

him: the tax collector stands for his followers, the Pharisee for his opponents. Jesus makes it plain what God is looking for.

else, Jesus told this parable: [10]"Two men went up
to the temple to pray, one a Pharisee and the
other a tax collector. [11]The Pharisee stood up
and prayed about himself: 'God, I thank you that
I am not like other men—robbers, evildoers,
adulterers—or even like this tax collector. [12]I
fast twice a week and give a tenth of all I get.'

[13]"But the tax collector stood at a distance. He
would not even look up to heaven, but beat his
breast and said, 'God, have mercy on me, a sin-
ner.'

[14]"I tell you that this man, rather than the
other, went home justified before God. For
everyone who exalts himself will be humbled,
and he who humbles himself will be exalted."

The Little Children and Jesus

Little children are at the heart of God's kingdom.

[15]People were also bringing babies to Jesus to
have him touch them. When the disciples saw
this, they rebuked them. [16]But Jesus called the
children to him and said, "Let the little children
come to me, and do not hinder them, for the
kingdom of God belongs to such as these. [17]I tell
you the truth, anyone who will not receive the
kingdom of God like a little child will never
enter it."

The Rich Ruler

By contrast, a wealthy young ruler cannot face up to the cost of following Jesus: he is a prisoner of his own possessions.

[18]A certain ruler asked him, "Good teacher,
what must I do to inherit eternal life?"

[19]"Why do you call me good?" Jesus answered.
"No-one is good—except God alone. [20]You
know the commandments: 'Do not commit adul-
tery, do not murder, do not steal, do not give false
testimony, honour your father and mother.'"

21"All these I have kept since I was a boy," he said.

22When Jesus heard this, he said to him, "You still lack one thing. Sell everything you have and give to the poor, and you will have treasure in heaven. Then come, follow me."

23When he heard this, he became very sad,
because he was a man of great wealth. 24Jesus
looked at him and said, "How hard it is for the
rich to enter the kingdom of God! 25Indeed, it is
easier for a camel to go through the eye of a needle than for a rich man to enter the kingdom of God."

26Those who heard this asked, "Who then can be saved?"

27Jesus replied, "What is impossible with men is possible with God."

28Peter said to him, "We have left all we had to follow you!"

29"I tell you the truth," Jesus said to them,
"no-one who has left home or wife or brothers
or parents or children for the sake of the king-
dom of God 30will fail to receive many times as
much in this age and, in the age to come, eternal life."

Jesus Again Predicts His Death

31Jesus took the Twelve aside and told them,
"We are going up to Jerusalem, and everything
that is written by the prophets about the Son of
Man will be fulfilled. 32He will be turned over to
the Gentiles. They will mock him, insult him,
spit on him, flog him and kill him. 33On the
third day he will rise again."

Jesus once again tells the disciples about his imminent betrayal and death.

34The disciples did not understand any of this. Its meaning was hidden from them, and they did not know what he was talking about.

A Blind Beggar Receives His Sight

Another of society's rejects experiences the healing touch of Jesus.

35As Jesus approached Jericho, a blind man
was sitting by the roadside begging. 36When he
heard the crowd going by, he asked what was
happening. 37They told him, "Jesus of Nazareth
is passing by."

38He called out, "Jesus, Son of David, have
mercy on me!"

39Those who led the way rebuked him and told
him to be quiet, but he shouted all the more,
"Son of David, have mercy on me!"

40Jesus stopped and ordered the man to be
brought to him. When he came near, Jesus asked
him, 41"What do you want me to do for you?"

"Lord, I want to see," he replied.

42Jesus said to him, "Receive your sight; your
faith has healed you." 43Immediately he received
his sight and followed Jesus, praising God.
When all the people saw it, they also praised
God.

Zacchaeus the Tax Collector

Yet another reject, of a different kind, finds that Jesus is on the lookout for him and is ready to rescue him from his life of extortion and robbery.

19 Jesus entered Jericho and was passing
through. 2A man was there by the name of
Zacchaeus; he was a chief tax collector and was
wealthy. 3He wanted to see who Jesus was, but
being a short man he could not, because of the
crowd. 4So he ran ahead and climbed a
sycamore-fig tree to see him, since Jesus was
coming that way.

5When Jesus reached the spot, he looked up
and said to him, "Zacchaeus, come down im-
mediately. I must stay at your house today." 6So
he came down at once and welcomed him gladly.

7All the people saw this and began to mutter,

"He has gone to be the guest of a 'sinner'."
8But Zacchaeus stood up and said to the Lord,
"Look, Lord! Here and now I give half of my
possessions to the poor, and if I have cheated
anybody out of anything, I will pay back four
times the amount."
9Jesus said to him, "Today salvation has come
to this house, because this man, too, is a son of
Abraham. 10For the Son of Man came to seek
and to save what was lost."

The Parable of the Ten Minas

11While they were listening to this, he went on
to tell them a parable, because he was near
Jerusalem and the people thought that the king-
dom of God was going to appear at once. 12He
said: "A man of noble birth went to a distant
country to have himself appointed king and
then to return. 13So he called ten of his servants
and gave them ten minas. 'Put this money to
work,' he said, 'until I come back.'
14"But his subjects hated him and sent a dele-
gation after him to say, 'We don't want this man
to be our king.'
15"He was made king, however, and returned
home. Then he sent for the servants to whom he
had given the money, in order to find out what
they had gained with it.
16"The first one came and said, 'Sir, your mina
has earned ten more.'
17"'Well done, my good servant!' his master
replied. 'Because you have been trustworthy in a
very small matter, take charge of ten cities.'
18"The second came and said, 'Sir, your mina
has earned five more.'
19"His master answered, 'You take charge of
five cities.'

Jesus provides the perspective of eternity as the context for our daily lives. We all have the opportunity to make our lives count for God. We will all be called to account by God.

[20]"Then another servant came and said, 'Sir, here is your mina; I have kept it laid away in a piece of cloth. [21]I was afraid of you, because you are a hard man. You take out what you did not put in and reap what you did not sow.'

[22]"His master replied, 'I will judge you by your own words, you wicked servant! You knew, did you, that I am a hard man, taking out what I did not put in, and reaping what I did not sow? [23]Why then didn't you put my money on deposit, so that when I came back, I could have collected it with interest?'

[24]"Then he said to those standing by, 'Take his mina away from him and give it to the one who has ten minas.'

[25]" 'Sir,' they said, 'he already has ten!'

[26]"He replied, 'I tell you that to everyone who has, more will be given, but as for the one who has nothing, even what he has will be taken away. [27]But those enemies of mine who did not want me to be a king over them—bring them here and kill them in front of me.' "

The Triumphal Entry

At the beginning of a week which will end in his crucifixion, Jesus rides on a donkey into the city of Jerusalem. He is acclaimed by his followers and the vast crowds, but targeted by the venom of the Pharisees.

[28]After Jesus had said this, he went on ahead, going up to Jerusalem. [29]As he approached Bethphage and Bethany at the hill called the Mount of Olives, he sent two of his disciples, saying to them, [30]"Go to the village ahead of you, and as you enter it, you will find a colt tied there, which no-one has ever ridden. Untie it and bring it here. [31]If anyone asks you, 'Why are you untying it?' tell him, 'The Lord needs it.' "

[32]Those who were sent ahead went and found it just as he had told them. [33]As they were untying the colt, its owners asked them, "Why are you untying the colt?"

34They replied, "The Lord needs it."
35They brought it to Jesus, threw their cloaks
on the colt and put Jesus on it. 36As he went
along, people spread their cloaks on the road.
37When he came near the place where the
road goes down the Mount of Olives, the whole
crowd of disciples began joyfully to praise God
in loud voices for all the miracles they had seen:

38"Blessed is the king who comes in the name of
the Lord!"

"Peace in heaven and glory in the highest!"

39Some of the Pharisees in the crowd said to
Jesus, "Teacher, rebuke your disciples!"
40"I tell you," he replied, "if they keep quiet,
the stones will cry out."
41As he approached Jerusalem and saw the
city, he wept over it 42and said, "If you, even you,
had only known on this day what would bring
you peace—but now it is hidden from your eyes.
43The days will come upon you when your
enemies will build an embankment against you
and encircle you and hem you in on every side.
44They will dash you to the ground, you and the
children within your walls. They will not leave
one stone on another, because you did not
recognise the time of God's coming to you."

Jesus at the Temple

45Then he entered the temple area and began
driving out those who were selling. 46"It is writ-
ten," he said to them, "'My house will be a
house of prayer'; but you have made it 'a den of
robbers'."
47Every day he was teaching at the temple. But

Now within the temple area, Jesus arouses the fury of the religious leaders by the way he attacks the commercialisation which is rampant in God's house.

the chief priests, the teachers of the law and the
leaders among the people were trying to kill
him. 48Yet they could not find any way to do it,
because all the people hung on his words.

The Authority of Jesus Questioned

His opponents attempt to undermine Jesus' authority.

20 One day as he was teaching the people in
the temple courts and preaching the
gospel, the chief priests and the teachers of the
law, together with the elders, came up to him.
2"Tell us by what authority you are doing these
things," they said. "Who gave you this authori-
ty?"
3He replied, "I will also ask you a question.
Tell me, 4John's baptism—was it from heaven, or
from men?"
5They discussed it among themselves and said,
"If we say, 'From heaven', he will ask, 'Why
didn't you believe him?' 6But if we say, 'From
men', all the people will stone us, because they
are persuaded that John was a prophet."
7So they answered, "We don't know where it
was from."
8Jesus said, "Neither will I tell you by what
authority I am doing these things."

The Parable of the Tenants

Jesus uses a story to throw into relief the issues at stake in the conflict between the religious authorities and himself.

9He went on to tell the people this parable: "A
man planted a vineyard, rented it to some farm-
ers and went away for a long time. 10At harvest
time he sent a servant to the tenants so they
would give him some of the fruit of the vineyard.
But the tenants beat him and sent him away
empty-handed. 11He sent another servant, but
that one also they beat and treated shamefully
and sent away empty-handed. 12He sent still a

third, and they wounded him and threw him
out.
13"Then the owner of the vineyard said,
'What shall I do? I will send my son, whom I
love; perhaps they will respect him.'
14"But when the tenants saw him, they talked
the matter over. 'This is the heir,' they said.
'Let's kill him, and the inheritance will be ours.'
15So they threw him out of the vineyard and
killed him.
"What then will the owner of the vineyard do
to them? 16He will come and kill those tenants
and give the vineyard to others."
When the people heard this, they said, "May
this never be!"
17Jesus looked directly at them and asked,
"Then what is the meaning of that which is writ-
ten:

"'The stone the builders rejected
has become the capstone'?

18Everyone who falls on that stone will be bro-
ken to pieces, but he on whom it falls will be
crushed."
19The teachers of the law and the chief priests
looked for a way to arrest him immediately,
because they knew he had spoken this parable
against them. But they were afraid of the people.

Paying Taxes to Caesar

20Keeping a close watch on him, they sent
spies, who pretended to be honest. They hoped
to catch Jesus in something he said so that they
might hand him over to the power and authori-
ty of the governor. 21So the spies questioned
him: "Teacher, we know that you speak and

Further attempts to catch Jesus out in his talk, in order to bring charges against him which could be sustained before the Roman governor.

teach what is right, and that you do not show partiality but teach the way of God in accordance with the truth. 22Is it right for us to pay taxes to Caesar or not?"

23He saw through their duplicity and said to them, 24"Show me a denarius. Whose portrait and inscription are on it?"

25"Caesar's," they replied.

He said to them, "Then give to Caesar what is Caesar's, and to God what is God's."

26They were unable to trap him in what he had said there in public. And astonished by his answer, they became silent.

The Resurrection and Marriage

The Sadducees (arch-rivals of the Pharisees) join in this orchestrated onslaught on Jesus.

27Some of the Sadducees, who say there is no resurrection, came to Jesus with a question. 28"Teacher," they said, "Moses wrote for us that if a man's brother dies and leaves a wife but no children, the man must marry the widow and have children for his brother. 29Now there were seven brothers. The first one married a woman and died childless. 30The second 31and then the third married her, and in the same way the seven died, leaving no children. 32Finally, the woman died too. 33Now then, at the resurrection whose wife will she be, since the seven were married to her?"

34Jesus replied, "The people of this age marry and are given in marriage. 35But those who are considered worthy of taking part in that age and in the resurrection from the dead will neither marry nor be given in marriage, 36and they can no longer die; for they are like the angels. They are God's children, since they are children of the resurrection. 37But in the account of the bush, even Moses showed that the dead rise, for he

calls the Lord 'the God of Abraham, and the
God of Isaac, and the God of Jacob'. [38]He is not
the God of the dead, but of the living, for to him
all are alive."
[39]Some of the teachers of the law responded,
"Well said, teacher!" [40]And no-one dared to ask
him any more questions.

Whose Son Is the Christ?

[41]Then Jesus said to them, "How is it that they
say the Christ is the Son of David? [42]David him-
self declares in the Book of Psalms:

"'The Lord said to my Lord:
"Sit at my right hand
[43]until I make your enemies
a footstool for your feet."'

[44]David calls him 'Lord'. How then can he be his
son?"
[45]While all the people were listening, Jesus
said to his disciples, [46]"Beware of the teachers of
the law. They like to walk around in flowing
robes and love to be greeted in the market-
places and have the most important seats in the
synagogues and the places of honour at ban-
quets. [47]They devour widows' houses and for a
show make lengthy prayers. Such men will be
punished most severely."

Jesus repeatedly confounds attempts to trip him up. He again warns the crowds against these religious leaders.

The Widow's Offering

21 As he looked up, Jesus saw the rich
putting their gifts into the temple treas-
ury. [2]He also saw a poor widow put in two very
small copper coins. [3]"I tell you the truth," he
said, "this poor widow has put in more than all

Jesus points out the way God looks at the money we give away: he counts what we give and he counts what we keep for ourselves.

the others. 4All these people gave their gifts out of their wealth; but she out of her poverty put in all she had to live on."

Signs of the End of the Age

Jesus talks at some length about two climactic events: the destruction of Jerusalem in his own generation (it took place in AD 70), and the end of this world as we know it.

5Some of his disciples were remarking about how the temple was adorned with beautiful stones and with gifts dedicated to God. But Jesus said, 6"As for what you see here, the time will come when not one stone will be left on another; every one of them will be thrown down."

7"Teacher," they asked, "when will these things happen? And what will be the sign that they are about to take place?"

8He replied: "Watch out that you are not deceived. For many will come in my name, claiming, 'I am he,' and 'The time is near.' Do not follow them. 9When you hear of wars and revolutions, do not be frightened. These things must happen first, but the end will not come right away."

10Then he said to them: "Nation will rise against nation, and kingdom against kingdom. 11There will be great earthquakes, famines and pestilences in various places, and fearful events and great signs from heaven.

12"But before all this, they will lay hands on you and persecute you. They will deliver you to synagogues and prisons, and you will be brought before kings and governors, and all on account of my name. 13This will result in your being witnesses to them. 14But make up your mind not to worry beforehand how you will defend yourselves. 15For I will give you words and wisdom that none of your adversaries will be able to resist or contradict. 16You will be betrayed even by parents, brothers, relatives and friends, and

they will put some of you to death. [17]All men will
hate you because of me. [18]But not a hair of your
head will perish. [19]By standing firm you will gain
life.

[20]"When you see Jerusalem being surrounded
by armies, you will know that its desolation is
near. [21]Then let those who are in Judea flee to
the mountains, let those in the city get out, and
let those in the country not enter the city. [22]For
this is the time of punishment in fulfilment of all
that has been written. [23]How dreadful it will be
in those days for pregnant women and nursing
mothers! There will be great distress in the land
and wrath against this people. [24]They will fall by
the sword and will be taken as prisoners to all the
nations. Jerusalem will be trampled on by the
Gentiles until the times of the Gentiles are ful-
filled.

Events which will indicate that the end of the world is near and that God's kingdom is about to be finally revealed, as the Son of Man comes in power and glory.

[25]"There will be signs in the sun, moon and
stars. On the earth, nations will be in anguish
and perplexity at the roaring and tossing of the
sea. [26]Men will faint from terror, apprehensive
of what is coming on the world, for the heavenly
bodies will be shaken. [27]At that time they will see
the Son of Man coming in a cloud with power
and great glory. [28]When these things begin to
take place, stand up and lift up your heads,
because your redemption is drawing near."

[29]He told them this parable: "Look at the fig-
tree and all the trees. [30]When they sprout leaves,
you can see for yourselves and know that sum-
mer is near. [31]Even so, when you see these things
happening, you know that the kingdom of God
is near.

[32]"I tell you the truth, this generation will cer-
tainly not pass away until all these things have
happened. [33]Heaven and earth will pass away,

but my words will never pass away.

Be careful.
Be watchful.
Be prayerful.

34“Be careful, or your hearts will be weighed
down with dissipation, drunkenness and the
anxieties of life, and that day will close on you
unexpectedly like a trap. 35For it will come upon
all those who live on the face of the whole earth.
36Be always on the watch, and pray that you may
be able to escape all that is about to happen, and
that you may be able to stand before the Son of
Man.”
37Each day Jesus was teaching at the temple,
and each evening he went out to spend the night
on the hill called the Mount of Olives, 38and all
the people came early in the morning to hear
him at the temple.

Judas Agrees to Betray Jesus

Judas decides to take the money offered by the religious leaders and sets out to betray Jesus.

22 Now the Feast of Unleavened Bread,
called the Passover, was approaching,
2and the chief priests and the teachers of the law
were looking for some way to get rid of Jesus, for
they were afraid of the people. 3Then Satan
entered Judas, called Iscariot, one of the Twelve.
4And Judas went to the chief priests and the offi-
cers of the temple guard and discussed with
them how he might betray Jesus. 5They were
delighted and agreed to give him money. 6He
consented, and watched for an opportunity to
hand Jesus over to them when no crowd was pre-
sent.

The Last Supper

Jesus gathers his friends for a Passover meal on Thursday night in an upper room in Jerusalem.

7Then came the day of Unleavened Bread on
which the Passover lamb had to be sacrificed.
8Jesus sent Peter and John, saying, “Go and

make preparations for us to eat the Passover."

9"Where do you want us to prepare for it?" they asked.

10He replied, "As you enter the city, a man carrying a jar of water will meet you. Follow him to the house that he enters, 11and say to the owner of the house, 'The Teacher asks: Where is the guest room, where I may eat the Passover with my disciples?' 12He will show you a large upper room, all furnished. Make preparations there."

13They left and found things just as Jesus had told them. So they prepared the Passover.

Jesus gives the Passover meal new meaning by linking it with his own death. He instructs the disciples to remember him in this way.

14When the hour came, Jesus and his apostles reclined at the table. 15And he said to them, "I have eagerly desired to eat this Passover with you before I suffer. 16For I tell you, I will not eat it again until it finds fulfilment in the kingdom of God."

17After taking the cup, he gave thanks and said, "Take this and divide it among you. 18For I tell you I will not drink again of the fruit of the vine until the kingdom of God comes."

19And he took bread, gave thanks and broke it, and gave it to them, saying, "This is my body given for you; do this in remembrance of me."

20In the same way, after the supper he took the cup, saying, "This cup is the new covenant in my blood, which is poured out for you. 21But the hand of him who is going to betray me is with mine on the table. 22The Son of Man will go as it has been decreed, but woe to that man who betrays him." 23They began to question among themselves which of them it might be who would do this.

The disciples argue with one another about who is the greatest among them.

24Also a dispute arose among them as to which of them was considered to be greatest. 25Jesus said to them, "The kings of the Gentiles lord it

over them; and those who exercise authority
over them call themselves Benefactors. 26But
you are not to be like that. Instead, the greatest
among you should be like the youngest, and the
one who rules like the one who serves. 27For who
is greater, the one who is at the table or the one
who serves? Is it not the one who is at the table?
But I am among you as one who serves. 28You are
those who have stood by me in my trials. 29And I
confer on you a kingdom, just as my Father con-
ferred one on me, 30so that you may eat and
drink at my table in my kingdom and sit on
thrones, judging the twelve tribes of Israel.

Jesus warns Simon Peter about the special pressure he is to face and about his collapse.

31"Simon, Simon, Satan has asked to sift you as
wheat. 32But I have prayed for you, Simon, that
your faith may not fail. And when you have
turned back, strengthen your brothers."

33But he replied, "Lord, I am ready to go with
you to prison and to death."

34Jesus answered, "I tell you, Peter, before the
cock crows today, you will deny three times that
you know me."

35Then Jesus asked them, "When I sent you
without purse, bag or sandals, did you lack any-
thing?"

"Nothing," they answered.

36He said to them, "But now if you have a
purse, take it, and also a bag; and if you don't
have a sword, sell your cloak and buy one. 37It is
written: 'And he was numbered with the trans-
gressors'; and I tell you that this must be fulfilled
in me. Yes, what is written about me is reaching
its fulfilment."

38The disciples said, "See, Lord, here are two
swords."

"That is enough," he replied.

Jesus Prays on the Mount of Olives

39 Jesus went out as usual to the Mount of
Olives, and his disciples followed him. 40 On
reaching the place, he said to them, "Pray that
you will not fall into temptation." 41 He with-
drew about a stone's throw beyond them, knelt
down and prayed, 42 "Father, if you are willing,
take this cup from me; yet not my will, but yours
be done." 43 An angel from heaven appeared to
him and strengthened him. 44 And being in
anguish, he prayed more earnestly, and his sweat
was like drops of blood falling to the ground.
45 When he rose from prayer and went back to
the disciples, he found them asleep, exhausted
from sorrow. 46 "Why are you sleeping?" he
asked them. "Get up and pray so that you will
not fall into temptation."

Leaving the upper room, Jesus goes to pray for strength to go through with God's will for him.

Jesus Arrested

47 While he was still speaking a crowd came up,
and the man who was called Judas, one of the
Twelve, was leading them. He approached Jesus
to kiss him, 48 but Jesus asked him, "Judas, are
you betraying the Son of Man with a kiss?"
49 When Jesus' followers saw what was going
to happen, they said, "Lord, should we strike
with our swords?" 50 And one of them struck the
servant of the high priest, cutting off his right
ear.
51 But Jesus answered, "No more of this!" And
he touched the man's ear and healed him.
52 Then Jesus said to the chief priests, the offi-
cers of the temple guard, and the elders, who
had come for him, "Am I leading a rebellion,
that you have come with swords and clubs?
53 Every day I was with you in the temple courts,

Judas arrives, leading a group of soldiers from the high priest. They are about to seize Jesus, when Peter lashes out with his sword and lops off the ear of one of them. Jesus rebukes Peter, heals the man's ear and speaks to the soldiers.

and you did not lay a hand on me. But this is your hour—when darkness reigns."

Peter Disowns Jesus

Jesus is led away to the high priest. Peter follows at a distance into the courtyard, where he is challenged and then denies three times that he knows Jesus.

[54]Then seizing him, they led him away and took him into the house of the high priest. Peter followed at a distance. [55]But when they had kindled a fire in the middle of the courtyard and had sat down together, Peter sat down with them. [56]A servant girl saw him seated there in the firelight. She looked closely at him and said, "This man was with him."

[57]But he denied it. "Woman, I don't know him," he said.

[58]A little later someone else saw him and said, "You also are one of them."

"Man, I am not!" Peter replied.

[59]About an hour later another asserted, "Certainly this fellow was with him, for he is a Galilean."

[60]Peter replied, "Man, I don't know what you're talking about!" Just as he was speaking, the cock crowed. [61]The Lord turned and looked straight at Peter. Then Peter remembered the word the Lord had spoken to him: "Before the cock crows today, you will disown me three times." [62]And he went outside and wept bitterly.

The Soldiers Mock Jesus

Jesus is mocked.

[63]The men who were guarding Jesus began mocking and beating him. [64]They blindfolded him and demanded, "Prophesy! Who hit you?" [65]And they said many other insulting things to him.

Jesus Before Pilate and Herod

66 At daybreak the council of the elders of the
people, both the chief priests and teachers of the
law, met together, and Jesus was led before
them. 67 "If you are the Christ," they said, "tell
us."

Jesus is examined as to his true identity. He affirms that he is the Son of God.

Jesus answered, "If I tell you, you will not
believe me, 68 and if I asked you, you would not
answer. 69 But from now on, the Son of Man will
be seated at the right hand of the mighty God."
70 They all asked, "Are you then the Son of
God?"
He replied, "You are right in saying I am."
71 Then they said, "Why do we need any more
testimony? We have heard it from his own lips."

23 Then the whole assembly rose and led
him off to Pilate. 2 And they began to
accuse him, saying, "We have found this man
subverting our nation. He opposes payment of
taxes to Caesar and claims to be Christ, a king."
3 So Pilate asked Jesus, "Are you the king of the
Jews?"

Taken to the Roman governor, Pilate, Jesus impresses him with his innocence of the accusations levelled at him.

"Yes, it is as you say," Jesus replied.
4 Then Pilate announced to the chief priests
and the crowd, "I find no basis for a charge
against this man."
5 But they insisted, "He stirs up the people all
over Judea by his teaching. He started in Galilee
and has come all the way here."
6 On hearing this, Pilate asked if the man was a
Galilean. 7 When he learned that Jesus was
under Herod's jurisdiction, he sent him to
Herod, who was also in Jerusalem at that time.
8 When Herod saw Jesus, he was greatly
pleased, because for a long time he had been
wanting to see him. From what he had heard
about him, he hoped to see him perform some

Herod, the Jewish king of the time, also puts many questions to Jesus.

miracle. [9]He plied him with many questions, but
Jesus gave him no answer. [10]The chief priests
and the teachers of the law were standing there,
vehemently accusing him. [11]Then Herod and
his soldiers ridiculed and mocked him. Dressing
him in an elegant robe, they sent him back to
Pilate. [12]That day Herod and Pilate became
friends—before this they had been enemies.

Back with Pilate, Jesus again is pronounced innocent of the charges brought against him. But Pilate wants to please the crowd. He bows to their cries for Jesus to be crucified.

[13]Pilate called together the chief priests, the
rulers and the people, [14]and said to them, "You
brought me this man as one who was inciting the
people to rebellion. I have examined him in your
presence and have found no basis for your
charges against him. [15]Neither has Herod, for
he sent him back to us; as you can see, he has
done nothing to deserve death. [16]Therefore, I
will punish him and then release him."

[18]With one voice they cried out, "Away with
this man! Release Barabbas to us!" ([19]Barabbas
had been thrown into prison for an insurrection
in the city, and for murder.)

[20]Wanting to release Jesus, Pilate appealed to
them again. [21]But they kept shouting, "Crucify
him! Crucify him!"

[22]For the third time he spoke to them: "Why?
What crime has this man committed? I have
found in him no grounds for the death penalty.
Therefore I will have him punished and then
release him."

[23]But with loud shouts they insistently
demanded that he be crucified, and their shouts
prevailed. [24]So Pilate decided to grant their
demand. [25]He released the man who had been
thrown into prison for insurrection and murder,
the one they asked for, and surrendered Jesus to
their will.

The Crucifixion

26As they led him away, they seized Simon
from Cyrene, who was on his way in from the
country, and put the cross on him and made him
carry it behind Jesus. 27A large number of peo-
ple followed him, including women who
mourned and wailed for him. 28Jesus turned and
said to them, "Daughters of Jerusalem, do not
weep for me; weep for yourselves and for your
children. 29For the time will come when you will
say, 'Blessed are the barren women, the wombs
that never bore and the breasts that never
nursed!' 30Then

Jesus is taken away to be crucified. Luke describes the reactions of different people as Jesus proceeds to the place of execution and is put on the cross.

> "'they will say to the mountains, "Fall on us!"
> and to the hills "Cover us!"'

31For if men do these things when the tree is
green, what will happen when it is dry?"
32Two other men, both criminals, were also
led out with him to be executed. 33When they
came to the place called the Skull, there they
crucified him, along with the criminals—one on
his right, the other on his left. 34Jesus said,
"Father, forgive them, for they do not know
what they are doing." And they divided up his
clothes by casting lots.
35The people stood watching, and the rulers
even sneered at him. They said, "He saved
others; let him save himself if he is the Christ of
God, the Chosen One."
36The soldiers also came up and mocked him.
They offered him wine vinegar 37and said, "If
you are the king of the Jews, save yourself."
38There was a written notice above him,
which read: THIS IS THE KING OF THE JEWS.
39One of the criminals who hung there hurled

insults at him: "Aren't you the Christ? Save
yourself and us!"
40But the other criminal rebuked him. "Don't
you fear God," he said, "since you are under the
same sentence? 41We are punished justly, for we
are getting what our deeds deserve. But this man
has done nothing wrong."
42Then he said, "Jesus, remember me when
you come into your kingdom."
43Jesus answered him, "I tell you the truth,
today you will be with me in paradise."

Jesus' Death

As Jesus breathes his last, strange events take place.

44It was now about the sixth hour, and dark-
ness came over the whole land until the ninth
hour, 45for the sun stopped shining. And the cur-
tain of the temple was torn in two. 46Jesus called
out with a loud voice, "Father, into your hands I
commit my spirit." When he had said this, he
breathed his last.
47The centurion, seeing what had happened,
praised God and said, "Surely this was a right-
eous man." 48When all the people who had gath-
ered to witness this sight saw what took place,
they beat their breasts and went away. 49But all
those who knew him, including the women who
had followed him from Galilee, stood at a dis-
tance, watching these things.

Jesus' Burial

Late on that Friday, Joseph of Arimathea gives Jesus a decent burial in his own, unused tomb.

50Now there was a man named Joseph, a mem-
ber of the Council, a good and upright man,
51who had not consented to their decision and
action. He came from the Judean town of Ari-
mathea and he was waiting for the kingdom of
God. 52Going to Pilate, he asked for Jesus' body.

[53]Then he took it down, wrapped it in linen
cloth and placed it in a tomb cut in the rock, one
in which no-one had yet been laid. [54]It was
Preparation Day, and the Sabbath was about to
begin.

[55]The women who had come with Jesus from
Galilee followed Joseph and saw the tomb and
how his body was laid in it. [56]Then they went
home and prepared spices and perfumes. But
they rested on the Sabbath in obedience to the
commandment.

The Resurrection

24 On the first day of the week, very early in
the morning, the women took the spices
they had prepared and went to the tomb. [2]They
found the stone rolled away from the tomb, [3]but
when they entered, they did not find the body of
the Lord Jesus. [4]While they were wondering
about this, suddenly two men in clothes that
gleamed like lightning stood beside them. [5]In
their fright the women bowed down with their
faces to the ground, but the men said to them,
"Why do you look for the living among the
dead? [6]He is not here; he has risen! Remember
how he told you, while he was still with you in
Galilee: [7]'The Son of Man must be delivered
into the hands of sinful men, be crucified and on
the third day be raised again.'" [8]Then they
remembered his words.

Early on Sunday morning, a group of women go to Jesus' tomb. They find it empty but are addressed by two angels. The women are told that Jesus has risen from the dead.

[9]When they came back from the tomb, they
told all these things to the Eleven and to all the
others. [10]It was Mary Magdalene, Joanna, Mary
the mother of James, and the others with them
who told this to the apostles. [11]But they did not
believe the women, because their words seemed

The women tell the eleven disciples what has happened.

to them like nonsense. 12Peter, however, got up
and ran to the tomb. Bending over, he saw the
strips of linen lying by themselves, and he went
away, wondering to himself what had happened.

On the Road to Emmaus

On the Sunday afternoon, two other disciples are walking to a village called Emmaus. Jesus joins them but remains unrecognised – until they welcome him into their house and their eyes are opened.

13Now that same day two of them were going
to a village called Emmaus, about seven miles
from Jerusalem. 14They were talking with each
other about everything that had happened. 15As
they talked and discussed these things with each
other, Jesus himself came up and walked along
with them; 16but they were kept from recognis-
ing him.

17He asked them, "What are you discussing
together as you walk along?"

They stood still, their faces downcast. 18One
of them, named Cleopas, asked him, "Are you
only a visitor to Jerusalem and do not know the
things that have happened there in these days?"

19"What things?" he asked.

"About Jesus of Nazareth," they replied. "He
was a prophet, powerful in word and deed before
God and all the people. 20The chief priests and
our rulers handed him over to be sentenced to
death, and they crucified him; 21but we had
hoped that he was the one who was going to
redeem Israel. And what is more, it is the third
day since all this took place. 22In addition, some
of our women amazed us. They went to the
tomb early this morning 23but didn't find his
body. They came and told us that they had seen a
vision of angels, who said he was alive. 24Then
some of our companions went to the tomb and
found it just as the women had said, but him they
did not see."

25He said to them, "How foolish you are, and

how slow of heart to believe all that the prophets
have spoken! 26Did not the Christ have to suffer
these things and then enter his glory?" 27And
beginning with Moses and all the Prophets, he
explained to them what was said in all the Scrip-
tures concerning himself.

28As they approached the village to which they
were going, Jesus acted as if he were going fur-
ther. 29But they urged him strongly, "Stay with
us, for it is nearly evening; the day is almost
over." So he went in to stay with them.

30When he was at the table with them, he took
bread, gave thanks, broke it and began to give it
to them. 31Then their eyes were opened and
they recognised him, and he disappeared from
their sight. 32They asked each other, "Were not
our hearts burning within us while he talked
with us on the road and opened the Scriptures to
us?"

33They got up and returned at once to
Jerusalem. There they found the Eleven and
those with them, assembled together 34and say-
ing, "It is true! The Lord has risen and has
appeared to Simon." 35Then the two told what
had happened on the way, and how Jesus was
recognised by them when he broke the bread.

The two disciples immediately walk back to Jerusalem and tell the eleven what has happened.

Jesus Appears to the Disciples

36While they were still talking about this,
Jesus himself stood among them and said to
them, "Peace be with you."

37They were startled and frightened, thinking
they saw a ghost. 38He said to them, "Why are
you troubled, and why do doubts rise in your
minds? 39Look at my hands and my feet. It is I
myself! Touch me and see; a ghost does not have
flesh and bones, as you see I have."

Jesus suddenly appears in their midst. He tells them to touch him, to prove that it really is him and not a ghost.

[40]When he had said this, he showed them his
hands and feet. [41]And while they still did not
believe it because of joy and amazement, he
asked them, "Do you have anything here to
eat?" [42]They gave him a piece of broiled fish,
[43]and he took it and ate it in their presence.

[44]He said to them, "This is what I told you
while I was still with you: Everything must be
fulfilled that is written about me in the Law of
Moses, the Prophets and the Psalms."

Jesus explains the significance of what has taken place – both what had been predicted long before, and what is now about to happen.

[45]Then he opened their minds so they could
understand the Scriptures. [46]He told them,
"This is what is written: The Christ will suffer
and rise from the dead on the third day, [47]and
repentance and forgiveness of sins will be
preached in his name to all nations, beginning at
Jerusalem. [48]You are witnesses of these things.
[49]I am going to send you what my Father has
promised; but stay in the city until you have
been clothed with power from on high."

The Ascension

He tells them to stay in Jerusalem, until they are clothed with power from on high to become witnesses to him. In giving them his blessing, he is taken up to heaven.

[50]When he had led them out to the vicinity of
Bethany, he lifted up his hands and blessed
them. [51]While he was blessing them, he left
them and was taken up into heaven. [52]Then they
worshipped him and returned to Jerusalem with
great joy. [53]And they stayed continually at the
temple, praising God.